MISTAKEN IDENTITY

GOD'S ISRAEL VS.
THE JEWS

Pat Brooks

2 Chronicles 7:14
Box 1212
Fairview, NC 28730

Back cover photo of the author by Charlie Bass.

Mistaken Identity is a completely revised and shortened version of *Hear, O Israel,* originally published in 1981.

Second Edition, called *Mistaken Identity*

Published by:
2 Chronicles 7:14
P.O. Box 1212
Fairview, NC 28730

ISBN: 0-932050-12-3
Library of Congress Card Number: pending

Foreword

Who are God's true people — Israel? The Jews? The Church?

Never one to shrink from a controversial issue, Pat Brooks tackles this explosive subject with her customary zeal and incisiveness — presenting an excellent overview which sorts out facts from fantasy, reality from blatant propaganda.

Mistaken Identity is bound to ruffle many feathers, shake many weak foundations, and "offend" many whose preconceived ideas are based on myth-information.

Containing myth-shattering documentation which is generally hidden from Western society, *Mistaken Identity* should be read by all who are concerned with the worsening world situation.

— Des Griffin
   Author of *Fourth Reich of the Rich, Descent into Slavery?* & *Anti-Semitism & the Babylonian Connection*

Table of Contents

CHAPTER 1

With Friends like These, Who Needs Enemies?

America is a nation at war – and the War on Terrorism is just a small part of it. The major casualty of this war is Truth. God calls us to agree with Him. Satan presents a constant barrage of lies to us – often enforced by the media and "entertainment industry" of our time.

Truth is what God says about a thing. It is the same in all ages, under all conditions. It is found in His Word, the Bible. Those whom Satan deludes think they can improve on it, and that they do not have to obey it. Those who follow the evil leadings of the devil usually evolve to a place in their thinking where they have no room for God. An incident happened in the 1960's which showed how far God's enemies will go to get rid of His people.

One of the most widely believed myths of history is the "miracle" story of the Israeli victory over the Palestinians during the June 5th to 10th "Six-Day War" of 1967.

Fearless non-Zionist Jew Alfred M. Lilienthal reported, in his book, *The Zionist Connection,* "On June 5, 1967, Israel had attacked Egyptian airfields and thrown crack paratroopers against the Jordanian Legion in Jerusalem. Despite the stubborn resistance of the Legion, the Israelis captured Jerusalem on June 7 and completed their conquest of Jordan's West Bank on the 8th." [1]

Not only did the Jews attack the Palestinians and drive the survivors from their homes. At the same time they attacked an American ship in the Mediterranean, leaving "34 sailors dead and 171 injured, and the damaged ship adrift with no power, rudder, or means of communication." [2]

The American ship was the *USS Liberty,* an intelligence-gathering ship with no combat capability. There were a few light machine guns for defense. At 6 a.m. on June 8th, an Israeli plane, identified by the ship's crew as a French-built Noratlas transport, circled the ship slowly several times over an 8-hour period. At 10 a.m., two rocket-armed jets circled the ship three times. The crew watched them through binoculars. An hour later the Noratlas returned, flying 200 feet above the *Liberty,* whose Stars & Stripes were clearly visible because of a steady breeze that day. The ship's crew members and pilot waved at each other. The plane returned every few minutes until 1 p.m. By then, the *Liberty* had changed course and was heading west. [3]

At 2 p.m. three Mirage fighter planes, identified with their 6-pointed star, headed straight for the *Liberty,* their rockets destroying the forward machine guns. Captain William L. McGonagle sent his radio Mayday message to the 6th Fleet at 2:10, seconds before the Israelis wrecked the ship's antennae and silenced her radio. Soon Mystere fighters appeared, dropping napalm on the deck while they strafed the ship. The assault continued for 20 minutes. Afterward, the *Liberty* had 821 holes in her sides and decks – more than 100 of them rocket-size. [4]

When the planes left, three torpedo boats took over, firing five torpedoes, killing 25 sailors. Captain McGonagle ordered the remaining crew to prepare to abandon ship. As the men lowered liferafts into the water, the torpedo boats shot them to pieces. As crew members tried to extinguish napalm fires, one torpedo boat trained machine guns on rafts still on deck, destroying them all. Petty Officer Charles Rowley said, "They didn't want anyone to live." [5]

By 3:15 p.m. the last shot was fired, leaving the vessel a morgue – and needing a hospital for the 171 wounded. The one doctor on board was surely a great hero that day.

Within 15 minutes of the attack, fighters from the *USS Saratoga* were in the air "to destroy or drive off any attackers." But Admiral Donald Engen, captain of the *America,* later explained, "President Johnson had very strict control. Even though we knew the *Liberty* was under attack, I couldn't just go and order a rescue." Soon Defense Secretary Robert McNamara gave this order over Sixth Fleet radios: *"Tell the 6th Fleet to get those aircraft back immediately."* [6]

Soon after 3 p.m., an hour after *Liberty's* "Mayday" call, the White House approved a rescue mission. Planes from both carriers took off. But at the same moment, the Israeli government informed the U.S. naval attaché at Tel Aviv that its forces had "erroneously attacked a U.S. ship" after "mistaking" it for an Egyptian vessel, offering "abject apologies." *Johnson immediately canceled the order for help, and ordered the aircraft back to their carriers. The Liberty was deserted for 15 hours. The survivors worked all night to keep the wounded alive and the ship afloat.* [7]

Immediately, McGonagle and his men knew they had been betrayed. There was no possibility of mistaken identity, for their 5' x 8' flag was flowing in the wind in a stiff breeze. Officer of the Deck James G. Ennes had it replaced with a 7' x 13' one when the Israelis destroyed the standard flag by gunfire. He later testified that Captain McConagle "defied bullets, shrapnel, and napalm" during the attack despite injuries, and stayed on the bridge all night. "Under his leadership, the 82 crewmen who had survived death and injury had kept the ship afloat despite a 40-foot hole in the side and managed to bring the crippled vessel to safe harbor." (That happened in Malta June 14, escorted by a destroyer, the *USS David,* and a 6th Fleet tug). [8]

The morning of June 9 two U.S. destroyers arrived with medical and repair assistance. A helicopter took the wounded to a carrier hospital. Those with major head injuries were flown to a U.S.

Military Hospital in Germany. The severely damaged ship then proceeded to Malta, where a Navy court of inquiry was scheduled. The Israeli account of the tragedy was entirely false. The CIA had learned a day before the assault that the Jews planned to sink the ship, and informed the navy so that the Joint Chiefs could order it elsewhere. A message was sent, but evidently never received on the *Liberty.* It was *"misrouted, delayed, and not received until after the attack."* [9]

The official inquiry, conducted by Admiral Isaac Kidd, gave terrifying orders to the crew. "Answer no questions. If somehow you are backed into a corner, then you may say that it was an accident and that Israel has apologized. You may say nothing else." In other words, the survivors *were ordered not to tell the truth!*

The official report, when it was released, was a pack of lies.

The American press was nearly silent. "Only the Malta *News* dared print that 'the attack on the *Liberty* was no mistake.'" [10]

Three months later, columnist James Kilpatrick wrote: "During the past month, press service interviews with survivors of the attack have turned up a uniform conviction that the attack was deliberate. Sailors point to the morning-long aerial surveillance; the presence of the flag; the known configuration of the *Liberty*; her name in English on the stern…her slow progression in international waters. All these factors support the crew's conclusion that the assault was no accident…." [11]

Israeli author Zeev Schiff revealed the great "befuddle plan" had been planned by Moshe Dayan, who also called for a news blackout on Israeli victories to prevent a cease-fire by the USSR or the UN. The *Liberty* had been monitoring Arab and Israeli transmissions from her post off Gaza, keeping the Joint Chiefs of Staff updated on the overwhelming Israeli victory in Jerusalem and the West Bank. Information gathered by the *Liberty* might bring about a cease-fire, which Dayan did not want. [12]

Lilienthal tells of other facts which the Israeli state did not want the USA to know: "The observers on the *Liberty* discovered that while the Arabs failed to crack Israeli codes, the Israelis had

4

penetrated Egyptian and Jordanian codes as soon as the war began. Somewhere between Amman and Cairo,...the messages between King Hussein and President Nasser were intercepted, reconstructed, and passed by the Israelis without detection, a process called 'cooking.' The Israelis blocked the message from Cairo that advised King Hussein of the bad military situation on the Egyptian front, rewording it to misinform the king that three-fourths of the Israeli Air Force had been destroyed over Cairo and that he was picking up Egyptian jets raiding targets in Israel on his radar. (They were actually Israeli jets returning from the destruction of Egyptian airfields.)

"The Israelis continued to 'cook' messages to give the impression that the war was going well for the Arabs. They falsely informed the King that Egypt was counterattacking in Sinai and needed support in the form of attacks on Israel in the Hebron area, obliging him to withdraw his forces from the planned crucial offensive designed to cut Israel in two. The Egyptians were likewise misled, thinking that the Jordanians had made a successful attack in Hebron. They counterattacked during the early hours of June 8, ignoring a UN call for a cease-fire. Thus the Israelis gained enough time to seize all of the West Bank they wanted, to consolidate their gains in Sinai, and to move their troops right up to the east bank of the Suez Canal." [13]

Had Captain McGonagle not sent a Mayday message to the 6th Fleet as soon as the jet attack on the *Liberty* began at 2 p.m., June 8, our ship would have been sunk. Actually, the Israelis destroyed all communications seconds after the Mayday message went out, and radar showed them the American jets leaving from the 6th Fleet seconds later. That explains the "mistaken identity" excuse and "apology" from the Israelis seconds later, and how craven President Johnson's "fear of the Jews" was. He canceled the help and had the jets turned back in mid-air to their carrier! No wonder Johnson and McNamara are among the most despised leaders in our national history.

Late in 2003, A&E put on a prime- time television series about

5

the assassination of President Kennedy. They featured interviews with the woman who had been Johnson's mistress since she was 15 years old. He took *her*, not his wife, to a big party in Texas with major financial donors to his campaigns, and according to the mistress, told her those Kennedys would never shame him again, "after tomorrow." That was the day that President Kennedy was assassinated.

From that day until Johnson's death eight years later, his wife reported that President Johnson was in a deep depression. Although he had some medical help, no medication seemed to pull him out of it. We can only imagine how much worse it got after he allowed 34 men on the *Liberty* to die, and 171 to be seriously wounded. Yet when Johnson wrote his memoirs, *Vantage Point,* Paul Findley says he "continued the fiction that the ship had been 'attacked in error.' Although his signature had appeared on letters of condolence to 34 next of kin, his memoirs reported the death toll at only ten. He cited 100 wounded; the actual count was 171. He added, 'This heartbreaking episode grieved the Israelis deeply, as it did us.'…The commander-in-chief devoted only 16 lines to one of the worst peacetime naval disasters in history." [14]

Not only that. When it came time to award the Congressional Medal of Honor to Captain William L. McGonagle, it was not presented by the President, nor was the ceremony in the White House. Admiral Thomas L. Moorer, who had become chief of naval operations, was furious. He would have been absolutely wild if he had known that "the White House delayed approving the medal until *it was cleared by Israel.*" The Secretary of the Navy presented the medal in a small, quiet ceremony at the Navy Yard in Washington. Admiral Moorer said later…'The way they did things I'm surprised they didn't just hand it to him under the 14th Street Bridge.'" [15]

Soon after the disaster, Carl F. Salans, legal adviser to the Secretary of State, released "Israeli Preliminary Inquiry 1/67" for Under-Secretary Eugene Rostow. It was immediately classified *top secret,* to be kept that way until 1983. Item by item, Salans demonstrated that the Israeli excuse could not be believed.

"Preparing the report immediately after the attack, he relied mainly on the limited information in Admiral Isaac Kidd's court of inquiry file. He never heard Ennes, Golden, nor any of the principal witnesses. Yet he found enough there to discredit the document thoroughly." [16]

Lt. James M. Ennes, Jr., while recovering in a hospital from shrapnel wounds, read an Associated Press story about the disaster. It was full of disinformation, supplied by an Israeli reservist on one of the torpedo boats, Micha Limor. During the four months Ennes was bedridden in Portsmouth, Virginia, he collected information from his shipmates. He got government reports under the Freedom of Information Act, and after nine years, the full court inquiry – declassified in 1979 from being top secret. [17]

James Ennis' book, *Assault on the Liberty,* was published in 1980 – two years after he retired from the Navy. He blew the lid on the whole cover-up. Although it got rave reviews, the Israeli Lobby declared war on the book. Orders were lost, interviews were canceled, and California talk show host Ray Taliaferro had two calls threatening his life after interviewing Ennes for 2 hours. (He had withstood 500 protest letters attempting to pressure him into canceling the show, beforehand.) [18]

However, perhaps the worst aftermath of this atrocity was the absolute refusal of the government to properly honor the dead at Arlington National Cemetary. The markers over the graves of 6 *Liberty* crewmen read simply, "died in the Eastern Mediterranean." "No mention of the ship, the circumstances, or Israel." [19] A huge, united protest from the *Liberty* survivors produced a change on the markers: "Killed, USS Liberty," in 1982. [20]

What kind of people are these that can pretend to be our strongest "allies" in the Middle East, while they persist in the most outrageous, hostile acts and lies against us? Today, what they did to the *Liberty* would clearly be called an act of terrorism – unless certain people are paralyzed by "the fear of the Jews." Believe it or not, this is a Biblical term, used to describe the disciples of the Lord

Jesus in the three days after his death, before His Resurrection. *Afterward,* there was no such fear. Once they saw him alive, and the nail prints in his hands and feet, they never feared again.

No, the people who perpetrated the *Liberty* atrocity were determined unbelievers. It is a clear case of *Mistaken Identity.* The "Chosen People" myth has been believed for far too long, by far too many. Those of you who have assumed that America's Jews have been brought up knowing the Old Testament need to know the truth.

Judaism is not the religion of the Old Testament, but of the Talmud. The biggest delusion under which most contemporary Christians operate is that the Jews, as we do, base their faith on the scriptures. Here are some quotations about the *Talmud* from *Jewish* sources.

"Judaism is the spiritual way of life developed by the Jewish people....The distinction frequently occurs in modern literature between the Religion of Israel and Judaism." [21]

"...the rabbis of the past made *enactments that had the effect of abrogating a law of the Bible.*" [22]

"...*rabbis had the right to dispense with the performance of a positive Biblical law if they had a valid reason for so doing.*" [23]

Doubtless, some readers are reeling from what (to you) is an entirely unknown incident, and thinking whatever strange "mistake" was involved here, nothing similar has happened since.

Oh no? Think again. Remember the Jonathan Pollard spy case in the 1990's? This man was a federal employee of the U.S. government who had been spying for the nation of Israel for years, and using his wife to help him, at times. Despite loud protestations from the Israeli government, the couple were eventually prosecuted. The wife got a brief sentence, but the case against Pollard himself was so severe that in 1996 he was given a life sentence, with no possibility of parole. That did not stop the Israelis from trying to gain his release with constant pestering of our justice department.

Then, in early September of 2004, sniffs of a real story began hitting the news about a *current* Israeli mole in the Pentagon, or perhaps three. Interestingly enough, they followed the resignation of longtime CIA Director, George Tenet. He had been warning about an Israeli *Mossad* officer who was a Pentagon mole, since 1998. His information evidently fell on deaf ears, despite the fact that the information showed that Israel had stolen U.S. nuclear secrets.

Immediately the disinformation campaign began. The Israelis protested that it was no longer their "policy" to spy on us, not since the Pollard case! Yet the FBI has been investigating Pentagon insider Larry Franklin for a year, who is suspected of passing classified documents to the American Israel Public Affairs Committee (AIPAC), concerning Iran's nuclear progress. [24] Two Jewish workers under him are also being investigated, but trying to get their names from Fox News proved futile, because we had no time to write them down when we heard the original program.

AIPAC reportedly has 65,000 members, and is the most powerful of all the Israeli lobbies. It has friends in both major political parties and its reason for being is primarily to see that the open spigot of money to Israel never stops flowing and increases yearly. Most of the smaller lobbies follow their lead in letters to write, politicians to call, and other strategies of their advocacy.

The American Free Press of 9/13/04 had two stories on this matter: the lead, front-page one by Richard Walker, and other on page 6 by Michael Collins Piper. The first sentence of the latter is excellent: "The latest Israeli spy scandal is inextricably linked to the activities of the pro-Israel neo-conservative network that has dominated U.S. Mideast policy during the presidency of George W. Bush."

The same issue of this excellent paper reveals that Mordechai Vanunu, the nuclear technician who blew the cover on the Israeli nuclear arsenal in the Negev in 1986 (and who spent 18 years in solitary confinement until his release in April), seeks asylum in the U.S. He became a Christian 20 years ago, and was living in an Anglican Cathedral, where he is the bell ringer. He told AFP that he is in constant danger of being killed by Israeli zealots, and when he left the building, went only into Palestinian areas of East Jerusalem. He was incarcerated again by the Israelis in early November, 2004.

Why is this brave man ignored? Our country has had a policy of admitting folks persecuted elsewhere for years, whose lives are in danger. Let's write some letters and call some congressmen! We believe many would want to hear his story. What hypocrisy that America would start a war in Iraq (where there are no nukes) and ignore UN resolutions demanding Israel give up theirs! This is never even mentioned by our government!

The "neo-cons" are the folks we used to call "Zionists" two decades ago. But, like everything else about Israeli policy, that term became far too definitive. No, there must be a way to identify themselves to one another, but keep the general public in ignorance.

Before we conclude this chapter, are there any clues as to *why* the Israelis attacked the *Liberty,* since it was a deliberate act? Yes, there are. Alfred Lilienthal says, "What is patently clear under any theory is that had the Israelis been successful in sinking the *Liberty,* the atrocity would have been blamed on the Egyptians and produced a Pearl Harbor reaction in the U.S. When the first news of the *Liberty* attack reached the Sixth Fleet, so certain was American reaction that it was the Egyptians who had struck, that a squadron of jets was sent in a threatening sweep over Cairo as if in a preliminary to war." [25] In other words, Dayan was planning to start World War III by *sinking the Liberty, and blaming the Egyptians for it!*

Do you see why every Christian worldwide needs to praise and thank Almighty God for preventing that, by using the courageous Captain McGonagle to send a *Mayday* message seconds before the radio was knocked out by Israeli jets?

As these words are being written, we are nearing the end of a political campaign which has been very bitter. We have been Bush supporters, because of the desperate need to get pro-life judges and justices appointed. Yet the Democrats have stonewalled his appointments, not even allowing them an up-or-down vote by the full Senate. Several newscasts have said that this is the longest time in the history of this republic that there has been no vacancy on the Supreme Court. There are some wonderful Christians running for the U.S. Senate, but we have become very concerned about Bush, because of his constant foolish positions on the Israeli mess.

Toward the end of August, a Georgia voter asked the following question of *USA Weekend* reporter, *Lorrie Lynch:* "I've read that Sen. John Kerry is actually of Jewish descent. Is that the case?"

Her answer was, "Yes. About 15 years ago, Kerry learned that his Hungarian paternal grandmother was Jewish, and converted to Catholicism before emigrating. And just last year it was reported that his Czech paternal grandfather also converted, changing his name from Kohn to Kerry (after the Irish county)." [26]

Kerry's poll numbers dropped from that weekend on. There is a great deal of fear in this country that a Jewish person might gain the office of greatest control here. The rest of this book will show whether this is a rational fear, or an irrational one. As George Santayana once said, "Those who refuse to learn from history, are doomed to repeat it."

Finally, here is a quotation from my 1981 book, now out of print, *Hear, O Israel:* "(In 1979) a Christian patriot in North Carolina 'baby-sat' for a ten-year-old Jewish girl while her parents were out-of-town. At bedtime, she tried to pray with the child, who refused, saying, 'We pray differently from you.'

"Thinking the child meant that she would not pray in the name of Jesus, the woman said, 'I understand, dear. All we shall do is pray to our Heavenly Father for the safety of your parents, and ask Him to give you a good night's sleep as He watches over you.'

"The child still refused. Finally, after persistent questions from the Christian as to what she meant, the little girl said, 'We pray differently from you. I mean, we pray to *Lucifer.'*

"It is high time Christians understand that the *Talmud,* on which most modern Jewish religion is based, is not biblical at all. It is *cabalistic....*Basically, it is a system of ancient Jewish sorcery which features magic rites being derived from the numerical combina-

11

tions of Old Tesatment Scriptures! In other words, the cabalist cares nothing for what God says: only that he believes occult rites are hidden there." [27]

Christians, even leaders, who use the offensive term "Judeo-Christian," had better wake up soon and realize what a stench it is to our Holy God. Judaism is Talmudic. It has nothing to do with the Torah, or the Old Testament scriptures. In fact, the Pharisees' system which was written down in the 2nd to 7th century A.D., was the same system that the Lord Jesus condemned so strikingly in Matthew 23, John 8, and other passages of the New Testament.

Here are Almighty God's comments on the subject of using anything other than His Word, the Bible, as our "only infallible rule of faith and practice":

"Ye shall not add unto the word which I command you, neither shall ye diminish ought from it, that ye may keep the commandments of the LORD your God which I command you." (Deuteronomy 4:2).

And here is His warning about the eternal destiny of those who do it:

"For I testify unto every man that heareth the words of the prophecy of this book: If any man shall add unto these things, God shall add unto him the plagues that are written in this book. And if any man shall take away from the words of the book of this prophecy, God shall take away his part out of the book of life, and from the things that are written in this book." (Revelation 22:18 & 19)

How will Almighty God judge us if we continue to let his enemies get their way with us? After all, they are the most anti-Christ influence in our country. Will He permit America to remain free if "the fear of the Jews" dominates our public policy?

CHAPTER 2

Origin of Earth's War — and Preview of Calvary

Earth's war is a spiritual war. Some call it a "cultural war," but that is a euphemism, designed to disguise the real nature of the conflict. If George Orwell were alive today, he would probably update his "thought police" to "Politically Correct" or "PC police," who will not tolerate calling anything by its real name.

This war is as old as the Fall of Satan, which the late Donald Grey Barnhouse put between Genesis 1:1 and 1:2 in his book, *The Invisible War.* He said a good translation of Genesis 1:2, where the King James Bible says, *"And the earth was without form, and void"* would be *"And the earth became chaos."* This happened when Lucifer, the "shining one," rebelled against God, was thrown out of heaven, and became Satan (i.e., the adversary). Read about it in Isaiah 14:12-15 and Ezekiel 28:11-19. These are the only two places where his fall to earth is described in detail.

That was round one. Round two was in the Garden of Eden, where Almighty God created a perfect man – and took away a part of him, giving him his wife. The KJV says she was *"an help meet for him,"* while newer translations call her a "suitable helper."

Yet the PC crowd today speculate on when marriage began!

Some say a few hundred, or a few thousand years ago. The Bible makes it clear. The Creator made Adam (i.e. *man)* first, and then took something he would never get back any other way, and created his wife. Their union would produce children, and their lifetime commitment to each other would nurture these young ones. Then all could have wholesome lives, and "have dominion" over the rest of his creatures – God's words, not mine.

Can you hear the outrage of the PC crowd? These are the ones who would have us save the baby whales, yet think there is a *right to choose murder of the unborn baby humans.*

Round three of the Great Conflict was the Fall of man. Read Genesis 3 to get it all. My simple paraphrase just hits the high spots.

Satan in the serpent said to the woman, "Oh yeah? Has God said, you shall eat of every tree of the garden?" (He cast doubt on God's Word, and it worked so well, he has been doing that ever since!)

And the woman said, "We can eat everything here, except the fruit from that tree out in the middle. God has said, You shall not eat from that or even touch it, for you'll die if you do." (This must have happened soon after God created her, or she would have known that animals don't talk.)

"Oh no, you won't die! If you do, your eyes will be open, and you'll be like gods, knowing good and evil," said the one whom the Lord Jesus would call the father of lies.

Suddenly, the woman saw things Satan's way. Why, that fruit was good for food, easy on the eyes, and would make her wise, so she took it and ate and gave some to her husband, and he ate – and they didn't drop dead on the spot, either!

But – something was wrong. They felt awful, and were embarrassed because they were naked, so they picked some fig leaves and sewed them together, making aprons. Then they heard God's voice calling them, and they hid from Him.

Adam heard God calling, "Adam, where are you?"

"I heard your voice, and I was afraid, because I was naked. So I hid."

"Who told you that you were naked? Have you eaten of the tree I told you never to eat?"

Suddenly, Adam knew he *would not or could not take responsibility for his own actions.* A major symptom of his sin came up as a solution – the blame game. "The *woman* You gave to be with me, she gave me that fruit, and I ate it."

At first glance, Adam blamed his wife for his fall. But he was really *blaming God.* "The woman *You* gave me…"

Then, when the LORD God confronted her, "What have you done?"

"The devil tricked me, and I ate." More blame game.

Then God consigned the serpent the devil had possessed to slither in the dirt forever, before He spoke directly to Satan. [End of paraphrase]

"And I will put enmity between thee and the woman, and between thy seed and her seed; it shall bruise thy head, and thou shalt bruise his heel." [Genesis 3:15]

There it is, in one great verse: the whole of earth's destiny. God's first prophecy was a promise of great warfare between the Seed of the woman (and all in Him) and the seed of the serpent. Her promised descendant, the Redeemer, would give the death blow to Satan and all of his "seed," but the Seed of the woman would suffer a heel wound! On Calvary, the Savior would die, but be raised from the dead 3 days later.

This verse was to give hope to the otherwise lost, over the ages. For things had permanently changed. Man had sinned, and the principal of mortality had set in. The man and his wife and their family would never have the close fellowship with God they had known, in their perfect state.

Furthermore, she was to pass on her sin nature to all her descendants of the human race – except one, the Lord Jesus Christ, who would be born of a virgin who experienced the immaculate conception. He inherited His Father's Divine Nature that way. Had it not been for the virgin birth, the Lord Jesus would have been *only* human like all the rest of us, and never could have saved us.

15

That is why it is so serious for anyone to reject Christ. The salvation the holy Son of God purchased with His own Blood was proven to be the Son of God when He rose from the dead. God has made *no other way.*

As a sign of that promise, the Lord God made coats of skins – thereby shedding blood – to clothe them, and make it possible for them to survive in what was now a very hostile world. For they could no longer stay in the garden, since they might eat of the Tree of Life. (Can we really imagine anything worse than their sin condition becoming *eternal?*)

No, sin changed everything. God made it clear that bearing children would be a dangerous matter. Eve's curse from God was, *"in sorrow shalt thou bring forth children."* [Gen. 3:16] She was to find that out with the birth of Cain, who killed his brother, Abel, in the field one day.

Because of Adam's sin, God said, *"Because thou hast hearkened unto the voice of thy wife, and hast eaten of the tree…cursed is the ground for thy sake; in sorrow shalt thou eat of it all the days of thy life. Thorns also and thistles shall it bring forth… In the sweat of thy face shalt thou eat bread, till thou return unto the ground; for out of it thou wast taken: for dust thou art, and unto dust thou shalt return."* [Genesis 3:17-19]

The rest of Genesis is much like the addressing of a letter. God promised a descendant of the first woman – in other words, a member of the human race. He would also be the Redeemer or Savior of her descendants – all who would believe among them.

"And Adam called his wife's name Eve because she was the mother of all living" [Genesis 3:20] – which was God's way of ending racism before it ever reared its ugly head. *"So He drove out the man; and He placed at the east of the garden of Eden Cherubims, and a flaming sword which turned every way, to keep the way of the tree of life."* [Genesis 3:24]

Then, many generations would pass before God indicated the family He had chosen to bring forth His Son – who would be the promised Seed of the woman.

First, in Genesis 12 God chose Abram (father) – at 75 years of age, with a barren wife ten years younger – to go "unto a land that I will show thee" and to be the father of the Hebrews! In other words, He made an impossible promise to a childless couple. All they had to do was *believe* it – and get moving!

Every crisis that this "friend of God" and his family faced for the rest of his life was one of faith. Would he believe God and do what He said? Or would he doubt, and get into big trouble? Read the rest of Genesis to find out how his family learned that.

We zero in on the biggest mistake God's servant ever made. He and Sarai (i.e., *contentious)* had been in the land of promise for over a decade, when she got a bright idea. She would give her handmaid, Hagar, to Abram to be his concubine, and would claim any son from the union as hers! It worked, in a way. Hagar got pregnant, but then she despised Sarai, who treated her harshly.

Hagar ran away; then *"the angel of the LORD found her"* and told her she must return to Sarai and submit to her. He also promised a son whom she was to name Ishmael. He told her she would have many descendants, and what they would be like. Then Hagar obeyed the angel, returned to Sarai, and submitted to her. When Abram was 86, Ishmael was born. [1]

When he was 99, Almighty God appeared to him again and changed his name to *Abraham* – *father of many nations.* He established His covenant with Abraham, promised him the land of Canaan, and commanded him to circumcise all males of his tribe or male servants, as a sign of that covenant.

Then God said, *"As for Sarai thy wife, thou shalt not call her name Sarai, but Sarah [i.e., princess] shall her name be. And I will bless her, and give thee a son also of her: yea, I will bless her, and she shall be a mother of nations; kings of people shall be of her."* [2]

Then Abraham laughed, as did Sarah, when she heard the news.

"And God said, Sarah thy wife shall bear thee a son indeed; and thou shalt call his name Isaac [i.e., Laughter]: and I will estab-

lish my covenant with him for an everlasting covenant, and with his seed after him. " [3]

Thus did laughter come into the lives of Abraham and Sarah in their old age, when God kept His impossible promise to them. A year after God appeared unto Abraham, Isaac was born, and by the time Sarah weaned him (probably at two years of age), his teenage half-brother mocked him.

Sarah saw it, and said to Abraham, *"Cast out this bondwoman and her son: for the son of this bondwoman shall not be heir with my son, even with Isaac."* [4]

Abraham loved Ishmael too, and grieved over the idea of losing him. But the Almighty intervened, and straightened him out.

"Let it not be grievous in thy sight because of the lad, and because of thy bondwoman: in all that Sarah hath said unto thee, hearken unto her voice: <u>for in Isaac shall thy seed be called.</u> And also of the son of the bondwoman will I make a nation, because he is thy seed. [5]

The very next morning Abraham sent Hagar and Ishmael away, with nothing but some bread and a bottle of water. It may sound strange, to our modern Western ears, that Abraham provided so little for his first son and his mother, but Almighty God was determined to have them trust Him and Him alone, for their provision. One can see that today, as Ishmael's descendants cry out, *"Allah is great!"* so often. This is not to say that the Muslim religion is right for them. No, the Lord God Almighty longs to bring them into His family through a relationship with His Son, the Lord Jesus Christ. This author prays that many of them will read this book and come to know Him here, as so many have this year, in seeing the film, *The Passion of the Christ.*

In any case, that life of trust began as soon as all the water in her bottle was gone.

"And God heard the voice of the lad; and the angel of God called to Hagar out of heaven, and said unto her, 'What aileth thee, Hagar? Fear not, for God hath heard the voice of the lad where he is. Arise, lift up the lad, and hold him in thine hand; for I

will make him a great nation.' And God opened her eyes, and she saw a well of water; and she went, and filled the bottle with water, and gave the lad drink." [6]

The Almighty was with Ishmael as he dwelt in the wilderness. When he grew up, his mother took him a wife out of the land of Egypt.

Sarah, Isaac's mother, lived 127 years until she died. That would make Isaac about 37 when he lost her. Then Abraham bought a burial place for her from Ephron for 400 shekels of silver, in the land of Hebron – on the West Bank, which is often in the news today. He could see that Isaac needed a wife, and did not want a heathen woman from the local area for that great calling. So he called his eldest steward, and made him promise he would get a wife for Isaac from the family of his brothers, who still lived in Haran.

When the steward got there, he prayed at the town's communal well, while the women of the area came to draw water, that the woman he asked to give him a drink would also offer to provide water for his camels – and that she would be the one for Isaac!

Read Genesis 24 for "the rest of the story," which is glorious history.

Please note the amazing blessing Rebecca's family gave to her as she left them to go and marry Isaac: *"Thou art our sister, be thou the mother of thousands of millions, and let thy seed possess the gate of those which hate them."* [7] That's *billions*, with a "b." And this incredible prophecy came from simple tribal people who had probably never seen a crowd of more than a few dozen in their lifetime.

Now, we flashback to Abraham, "the friend of God," and the great testing of his life – in Genesis 22, the pinnacle of Old Testament revelation – a preview of Calvary, fulfilled in the New.

Many years have passed since the events of Genesis 21. Isaac is "a lad" here – probably between 12 and 17 years of age – before his marriage, before losing either one of his parents. Abraham is very old, now. He could have easily been resisted by a strong teenager.

And it came to pass after these things, that God did tempt Abraham, and said unto him, 'Abraham': and he said, 'Behold, here I am.' And He said, 'Take now thy son, thine only son Isaac, whom thou lovest, and get thee into the land of Moriah; and offer him for a burnt offering upon one of the mountains which I will tell thee of.

"And Abraham rose up early in the morning, and saddled his ass, and took two of his young men with him, and Isaac his son, and clave the wood for the burnt offering, and rose up, and went unto the place of which God had told him. Then on the third day, Abraham lifted up his eyes, and saw the place afar off. And Abraham said unto his young men, 'Abide ye here with the ass: and I and the lad will go yonder and worship, and come again to you.'

"And Abraham took the wood of the burnt offering, and laid it upon his son: and he took the fire in his hand, and a knife; and they went both them together.

"And Isaac spake unto Abraham his father, and said, 'My father': and he said, 'Here am I, my son.' And he said, 'Behold the fire and the wood; but where is the lamb for a burnt offering?'

"And Abraham said, 'My son, God will provide himself a lamb for a burnt offering': so they went both of them together.

"And they came to the place which God had told him of; and Abraham built an altar there, and laid the wood in order, and bound Isaac his son, and laid him on the altar upon the wood.

"And Abraham stretched forth his hand, and took the knife to slay his son.

"And the angel of the LORD called unto him out of heaven, and said, 'Abraham, Abraham': and he said, 'Here am I.'

"And He said, 'Lay not thine hand upon the lad, neither do thou anything to him, for now I know that thou fearest God, seeing thou hast not withheld thy son, thine only son from me.'

"And Abraham lifted up his eyes, and looked, and behind him a ram caught in a thicket by his horns: and Abraham went and took the ram, and offered him up for a burnt offering in the stead *of his son. And Abraham called the name of that place 'Jehovah Jireh': as it is said to this day, 'In the mount of the Lord it shall be seen (or be provided).'" [8]*

This passage gives us some idea of what it was costing Abraham to obey God in this matter. It also reveals the heart of Almighty God – what He knew it was going to cost Him to see His Son die on Calvary! Be sure to read the rest of the passage (verses 15-18) to see the extraordinary blessings Abraham was promised because of this obedience.

But what did Abraham actually *believe,* in those agonizing seconds he held the knife in his hand, while Isaac lay abound upon the altar? The great "heroes of faith" chapter, Hebrews 11:17-19 tells us. He believed God would raise Isaac from the dead!

In other words, Abraham had *Resurrection Faith* – the same kind required of everyone who would ever receive eternal life after Jesus came, died for our sins, and rose from the dead! Romans 10:9 makes that completely clear.

In this incredible account, we see a picture of God the Father in Abraham, willing to offer up his one and only son. We see a type of Christ in Isaac, willing to be bound and offered up as a sacrifice, if that were the will of his father and of God. And in the words of Abraham, "God will provide himself a lamb," we see the gospel: the Father sending the Son to be "the lamb of God that taketh away the sin of the world." [9] And even the millions of us who wept our way through the film, "The Passion of the Christ," must realize – the real thing was far worse than that.

Jim Caviezel, the actor who played the Lord Jesus on the cross, did suffer there. He was struck by lightning twice while he hung there, and he was cold while others in warm clothing stood at the foot of the cross. But he did not really have the nails in his hands and feet, nor suffer the total separation from God His Father that the Lord Jesus experienced there.

"Surely He hath borne our griefs, and carried our sorrows: yet we did esteem him smitten Of God and afflicted. But He was wounded for our transgressions, He was bruised for our iniquities;

the chastisement of our peace was upon Him; and with his stripes we are healed. All we like sheep have gone astray; we have turned every one to his own way; and the Lord hath laid on Him the iniquity of us all." [10]

There is another scripture in the Old Testament that pictures Calvary. It is Psalm 22, which opens with the agonized cry of the Lord Jesus on the Cross: *"My God, my God, why hast Thou forsaken me?"*

Unlike the gospels of the New Testament, where others describe Christ's passion on the Cross, here in Psalm 22 we actually hear Him crying out to the One he always called "Father" at other times.

"I am poured out like water, and all my bones are out of joint: my heart is like wax; it is melted in the midst of my bowels. My strength is dried up like a potsherd; and my tongue cleaveth to my jaws; and thou hast brought me into the dust of death. For dogs have compassed me: the assembly of the wicked have inclosed me; they pierced my hands and my feet. I may tell [i.e., count] all my bones; they look and stare upon me

"They part my garments among them, and cast lots upon my vesture..." [11]

The witness of the Lord Jesus in Psalm 22 is one of the greatest proofs of the divine origin of scripture. No honest scholar denies its existence at least 800 years before it happened – and even 400 years before the Romans dreamed up the awful form of execution that was crucifixion!

We are told in our Bibles, in the heading beneath the number, that it is "a psalm of David" – the human author. But David was never crucified. He must have been amazed as the Holy Spirit poured out the words through him, in the past tense – as if it had already happened!

What the Son of God – who is also God the Son – did on the Cross of Calvary is mightily explained by a New Testament verse or two:

"For He hath made Him to be sin for us, who knew no sin, that

we might be made the righteousness of God in Him. [12]

"For God so loved the world, that He gave His only begotten Son, that whosoever believeth in Him should not perish, but have everlasting life." [13]

What of those who *refuse to believe?*

It is a risk no sane man or woman would ever take. How wonderful to know the Word says, *"Whosoever believeth that Jesus is the Christ is born of God."* [14]

CHAPTER 3

How Israel Began

The Bible is an amazing book. It is made up of 66 books, written by many different authors, over a period of 1500 years. It contains history, but its major theme is human redemption. It points out the Redeemer, our Lord Jesus Christ, and is His story.

We have seen that God chose the family that would bring forth His Son – the messianic line, which was the family of Abraham, Isaac, and Jacob/Israel. Of Jacob's two wives, God chose Leah to bear Judah. On his deathbed, the patriarch spoke to his 12 sons in Genesis 49. To Judah he prophesied, *'The scepter shall not depart from Judah, nor a lawgiver from between his feet, until Shiloh come; and unto him shall the gathering of the people be."* [1]

Bible scholars have agreed, over the ages, that "Shiloh" here refers to our Redeemer, the Lord Jesus Christ – King of kings, and Lord of lords.

The envelope is now almost addressed. To Eve, in the Garden of Eden in Genesis 3:15, she was told He was to be her descendant: a member of the human race. In Genesis 12:1-3, Abram was told, "in thee shall all families of the earth be blessed." The messianic family is identified. Then Isaac is born, 25 years later – a

25

miraculous birth. God would not allow Ishmael to remain in the household afterward. He could well have become a potential assassin, with his mother's and his great hatred and envy for Isaac.

Admittedly, God's choice of Leah, instead of Rachel, was somewhat unusual. But His choice of Judah's son through Tamar, his daughter in-law, was positively breathtaking. A very dear friend of this author explained Tamar's incredible behavior to me, decades ago. "She was going to get what was promised to her!"

Genesis 38 is a hard chapter to read. It does not present Judah, the chosen seed of Israel to produce the messianic line, in a good light. But lest we are tempted to judge Judah as a worse sinner than ourselves, we must remember that God is sovereign. It was His idea to send our Redeemer through the fallen human race to save them, not ours. Yet he protected His one and only Son through the virgin birth so that His Son would not inherit the inevitable propensity to sin that all the rest of us have.

One fact is obvious from the passage. Tamar is chosen to be in the messianic line. Perhaps her very persistence in demanding a child through Judah is a characteristic God found worthy to be in the human gene pool for His Son – who was to persevere through incredible suffering on His path to the Cross, and never to fail His Father when he was hanged there. My maternal grandfather used to say, "Remember the postage stamp, my child, and its ability to stick to one thing until it gets there."

We never hear of Tamar again, after she seduced her father-in-law, except in the passage of the line of David showing the earthly line of the Lord Jesus Christ. [Matthew 1:3]

But don't be embarrassed for God! He makes no mistakes. Thus, in the first chapter of the New Testament, after over 400 years of silence, He mentions her among women in the family line of the Lord Jesus – women who included both Rahab the harlot, Ruth the Moabitess, and Tamar, who pretended to be a harlot, in order to seduce her father-in-law and have the children he had promised her through his sons.

Thus we have in the very messianic line of our Lord Jesus Christ an ancestor, a woman of faith, who resorted to less than godly means

26

to get what God had promised for her.

In the patriarchal society of that time, the elder had two blessings that no later ones had: the birthright of a special relationship with their earthly father, and with God, their heavenly Father; and much greater wealth of inheritance than younger children.

The Bible describes the birth of these twin brothers in this way: *"And the first came out red, all over like an hairy garment; and they called his name Esau [i.e., hairy]. And after that came his brother out, and his hand took hold on Esau's heel; and his name was called Jacob* [i.e.,supplanter]

"And Isaac was 60 years old when she bare them." [2] That first act of his, at his birth, described his attitude toward his brother, as they grew up.

Once, after the twins were adults, Esau returned, famished from the hunt. He saw Jacob making a stew of red lentils, and asked his brother, *" 'Feed me, I pray thee, of that same red pottage, for I am faint.' Therefore was his name called Edom.* [i.e., red.]

"And Jacob said, 'Sell me this day thy birthright.'

And Esau said, "Behold, I am at the point to die, and what profit shall this birthright do to me?"

"And Jacob said, 'Swear to me this day'; and he sware unto him: and he sold his birthright to Jacob…Thus Esau despised his birthright." [3]

He gave it up for a mere meal, when he was hungry.

Genesis 27 deals with an even more contemptible act of Jacob – at his mother's urging. Rebecca hears Isaac call his son Esau to ask him to hunt for deer, and bring the venison, cooked, to him, that he might give him the blessing of his inheritance.

While her older son goes hunting, Rebecca calls Jacob, and puts him up to a despicable deception, based on the fact that Isaac is now blind, and thinks he is about to die.

She asks Jacob to bring two kids of the goats, to prepare meat as she knows Isaac loves, and put on his brother's clothes, that he may pretend to be Esau, and receive the firstborn's blessing of inheritance.

And Jacob said to Rebecca his mother, 'Behold, Esau my brother is a hairy man, and I am a smooth man. My Father peradventure will feel me, and I shall seem to him as a deceiver: and I shall bring a curse upon me, and not a blessing.

"And his mother said unto him, "Upon me be thy curse, my son: only obey my voice, and go fetch me them." ' [4]

The reader can finish this sad tale by reading the rest of Genesis 27. God's judgments fall on both Jacob and his mother – and the curse Jacob feared did, indeed, fall on Rebecca.

Esau is furious and vows to kill his brother Jacob. Rebecca again intervenes and gets Isaac to send Jacob to her brother Laban, to escape from Esau, and choose a wife from his family.

The self-pity and dire predictions of his death prove inaccurate for Isaac. He has decades yet to live, but Rebecca is never mentioned as alive again in the scriptural narrative. Her favorite son, Jacob, spends 20 years or so, not just a few weeks, working for the wily Laban and his 2 daughters – not just Rachel, whom he loved. It would be accurate to say that God cured the deceptive Jacob of his dishonesty by placing him under Laban, a far worse deceiver!

Yet, we are all sinners, as Romans 3:23 says. Therefore, one of the most comforting phrases in the whole Bible refers to the Almighty as "the God of Jacob."

We can all relate to that! If God loved Jacob, and saw him through many trials, there is hope for you and me.

Interestingly enough, the barren curse afflicts Rachel as it did Rebecca and Sarah before her. At one point she cries out to Jacob, *"Give me children, or else I die."* [5] Eventually, *"God remembered Rachel, and God hearkened to her,"* and Joseph was born. [6]

Joseph is one of the giants of Scripture. Greatly beloved of Jacob, he also was especially chosen by his heavenly Father for one of the key roles of His chosen family.

Soon after his birth, Jacob decides to return to his homeland, and face the wrath of Esau. He does not tell Laban, his father-in-law, that he is leaving, so the super-schemer chases after him. Im-

28

mediately, Laban accuses him of stealing his household gods: heathen images. Jacob reacts with great anger, and says whoever has them must die, not realizing that Rachel had stolen them. Rachel then puts them with the camel's furniture, and sits on them, apologizing that she cannot get up when her father looks in her tent, because *"the custom of women is upon me."* [7]

Later, when Jacob makes a pilgrimage to Bethel, Rachel dies during hard labor, bringing forth their second son, whom Jacob calls Benjamin. In the New Testament, Jesus says that *"Every idle word that men shall speak, the shall give account thtereof in the day of judgment."* [8]

Whether Rachel ever told Jacob about the idols is not mentioned in Scripture. But Jacob's rash words were heard by God, and honored by Him. This incident shows a great defect in Rachel's character.

This writer has always suspected this flaw was the reason the Almighty chose Leah as the mother of Judah, ancestor of the Lord Jesus, and allowed Laban to trick Jacob into marrying her first. We can be sure that the Father gave His Son the best genetic heritage available in the messianic family line!

We have mentioned that Jacob is ready to face the wrath of Esau on his return from Syria. He decides to placate him with gifts of oxen, donkeys, and flocks, and sends that word ahead, by messengers. They return with the news that his brother is coming to welcome him home – with 400 men!

At first, Jacob responds with typical scheming, since he is overcome by great fear. He divides all the livestock into two groups, saying, *"If Esau come to the one company, and smite it, then the other company which is left shall escape."* [9]

Then he prays. *"O God of my father Abraham, and God of my father Isaac, the LORD which saidst unto me, 'Return unto thy country, and to thy kindred, and I will deal well with thee: I am not worthy of the least of all the mercies, and of all the truth, which thou hast shewed unto thy servant; for with my staff I passed over this Jordan; and now I am become two bands. Deliver me, I pray thee, from the hand of my brother, from the hand of Esau: for I fear him, lest he will come and smite me, and the mother with the children. And thou saidst, 'I will surely do thee good, and make thy seed as the sand of the sea, which cannot be numbered for multitude.'"* [10]

That night Jacob put the gift livestock in front of the company; then he took his two wives, and their two maids, and his eleven sons, and passed over the ford Jabbok, sending them over the brook, with all he had. [11]

And Jacob was left alone; and there wrestled a man with him until the breaking of the day." [12]

Who was this man? Many think it was an angel, but some believe it was a Christophany – a pre-incarnate appearance of the Second Person of the Trinity, our Lord Jesus Christ. That was Jacob's own view, as a careful reading of Genesis 32:24 to 32 will show.

At any rate, Jacob could not be used by God until he was completely changed. The schemer had to be broken. When God touched the hollow of Jacob's thigh, he became lame, and apparently stayed that way the rest of his life. Then the one that wrestled with him told him, *"Thy name shall be called no more Jacob, but Israel: for as a prince hast thou power with God and with men, and hast prevailed."* [13]

There it is – the first mention in the Word of God of Israel, about which there is almost total misunderstanding on earth today. Perhaps we can shed a little light on this mystery, and God will dispel the confusion in our minds. But first we must lay aside our prejudices and our superstitions on this subject.

Then we can have a better idea of God's purpose for believers today.

Jacob became Israel after his 12th son, Benjamin, was born. The 12 tribes of Israel were named after the 12 sons, except in the case of Joseph, who had 2 sons, Manasseh and Ephraim – the two half-tribes. The answer to this puzzle may appear in the listing of the tribes in Revelation 7, where *Dan is missing.* Manasseh is mentioned, but here the other half-tribe, Ephraim, (10 times the size of

Manasseh) is simply called Joseph.

Two prophetic voices of Scripture speak of the destiny of the 12 tribes: Jacob, on his deathbed in Genesis 48 & 49, and Moses, just before he died, in Deuteronomy 33.

There are two sentences about Dan in the prophecy Jacob gave his sons in two verses of Genesis 49, verses 16 and 17. Verse 16 merely mentions a role that Dan shared with his brothers many times: The next comment, verse 17, is much more ominous: *"Dan shall be a serpent by the way, an adder in the path, that biteth the horse heels, so that the rider shall fall backward.* [14]

Ever since the Fall of man in the Garden of Eden, God only uses serpents in a negative way, to indicate the work of Satan. "Falling backwards" seems to be a picture of *backsliding* in Scripture. Jeremiah uses the term 14 times; Hosea, three times. Perhaps God is saying that Dan would cause many to backslide or even apostatize. One cannot be dogmatic about this, but it appears Dan was to do Satan's work for him. At any rate, in the listing of the sealed among the tribes, in Revelation 7, Dan is missing.

However, one thing is perfectly clear. There are 12 thousand of each of the 12 tribes, or 144,000, who are sealed in their foreheads, and Joseph is mentioned, rather than either Dan or Ephraim in Revelation 7.

The final point we must stress about Jacob's prophetic words to the tribes is his amazing dealings with Joseph's two sons, in Genesis 48, before the rest of the family is called in.

The first striking thing about this encounter is that Israel calls Ephraim and Manasseh "mine" just like Reuben and Simeon.

Then Jacob/Israel proceeds to bless them, but crosses his hands over to put his right hand on Ephraim; his left on Manasseh.

At this point, Joseph tries to object, and points out that Manasseh is the firstborn, and should have Jacob's right hand.

But his father refuses, and says, *"I know it, my son, I know it: he also shall be a people, and he also shall be great: but truly his younger brother shall be greater than he, And his seed shall become a multitude of nations."* [15]

31

Need we say, that in the above scene, Israel made the sign of the cross over his two grandsons? Were their descendants to be the major Christian tribes of Israel in the centuries ahead?

It was my privilege to have known the late Roger Rusk, retired professor of physics at the University of Tennessee, before he died. For the last five decades of his life, he studied the Bible, secular history, and archaeology to confirm to him that we, indeed, the Western peoples, are descendants of the northern tribes of Israel. He wrote a book on the subject, *The Other Side of the World*. Before that, however, he gave me two excellent tables which appeared as Appendices B and C of my book, *Hear, O Israel*, which was published in 1981. They are also at the end of this book.

However, in one of our many conversations on this fascinating subject, he told me a powerful fact: *The Septuagint*, the Greek translation of the Old Testament, had the same identical Greek phrase for "a multitude of nations" in Genesis 48:19, as appears in the New Testament, in Romans 11:15, and is translated "the fullness of the Gentiles." Thus, God Almighty himself identified the seed of Ephraim would be known to the world as *Gentiles*. The Greek plural of *ethnos* is, of course, *ethni*, from which we get our adjective *ethnic*. However, it is usually translated "Gentiles" or "nations" in the New Testament.

Think about that! Our God is big enough to have clearly identified His Israel people in the second millennium B.C. Yet contemporary Christians cannot seem to face the fact that they are of Israel, and not just grafted in! By far the worst fruit of this stubborn resistance to truth is the insistence of many of them to approve the imposters – many of those called "Jews" today.

Who *are* the "Jews"? It was not a word that appeared in the English language until 1775, when dramatist Richard Sheridan used it in his play, *The Rivals*, according to Benjamin Freedman, Jewish convert to Catholicism in his letter to David Goldstein, LLD, on 10/10/1954. [16]

This is not a small matter. Today we are being deluged with "translations" of later manuscripts which got into the hands of

32

men [Westcott and Hort] who admitted they *changed* things not to their liking – even in the inferior Alexandrian manuscripts they were using.

It is now important to examine *why* God divided the kingdom into Judah and Israel, and what happened to the northern kingdom.

CHAPTER 4

Why Did God Divide the Tribes into Two Kingdoms?

The subject of this chapter is deliberately set as a question – not because this author has any final answers to it, but to inspire a debate most have never considered.

Perhaps the best place to start is to point out how totally confused most believers are on the terms "Israel" and "the Jews" today. Dozens of times in my own lifetime this writer has heard the totally erroneous statement, "Abraham was the father of the Jews," – often from the pulpit!

No, he was the father of the Hebrews. There is a vast difference between the two. In fact, the *first* reference to "Jews" in the Bible is II Kings 16:6, shortly before the Assyrian Captivity. It is important to realize that the Hebrew plural for Jews is *Yehudim* (i.e., of Judah). That is the Old Testament term. The New Testament term is *Ioudaioi* – Greek for "of Judea" – a place, rather than a tribe of people.

Toward the end of King Solomon's reign, his 700 wives *"turned away his heart after other gods…and Solomon did evil in the sight of the LORD, and went not fully after the LORD, as did David his father."* [1]

God had promoted Jeroboam "over all the house of Joseph," [or ten northern tribes: the House of Israel – Ed.] Once, Jeroboam went out of Jerusalem, clothed with a new garment. The prophet Ahijah found him in a field, *"And Ahijah caught the new garment that was on him, and rent it in 12 pieces: and he said to Jeroboam, 'Take thee ten pieces, for thus saith the LORD the God of Israel, Behold, I will rend the kingdom out of the hand of Solomon, and will give 10 tribes to thee, (but he shall have one tribe for my servant David's sake, and for Jerusalem's sake, the city which I have chosen out of all the tribes of Israel.)'"* [2]

Then Jeroboam fled to Egypt until Solomon died.

Not long after Solomon died, and Rehoboam his son reigned in his stead, Jeroboam returned from Egypt, and came to see Rehoboam with a delegation from the northern kingdom of Israel. Their message was simple: "Your father put a heavy yoke on us; make it lighter, and we will serve you."

Rehoboam asked the old counselors who served his father what he should do. They told him to listen to the people, and they would be his servants forever.

Rehoboam then asked the young men who had grown up with him what they thought. His drinking buddies told him to say, *"I will add to your yoke: my father hath chastised you with whips, but I will chastise you with scorpions."* [3]

"Wherefore the king hearkened not unto the people, for the cause was from the LORD, that He might perform his saying, which the LORD spake by Ahijah the Shilonite unto Jeroboam the son of Nebat." [4]

The results were predictable. Rehoboam continued on in his delusion, even sending his tax-collector up north. They stoned the IRS man to death, and the king sped to his chariot, to flee to Jerusalem. However, once there, he determined to fight the northern kingdom in a war, until God sent a direct message to him by Shemaiah, a man of God:

"Thus saith the LORD, Ye shall not go up nor fight against your brethren the children of Israel: return every man to his house:

for this thing is from me." [5]

Rehoboam obeyed, and stopped the civil war. But the rest of the chapter is profoundly depressing, as Jereboam had golden calves made, for the people to worship, in Bethel and in Dan. The northern Kingdom of the House of Israel never had a good king, and went into the Assyrian captivity in 722 B.C.

The House of Judah was a bit better. It had some good kings, with many bad ones, culminating in the Babylonian Captivity. Then there was a period of over 400 years when no message came from God, after the Book of Malachi was written.

We evangelicals are told two gigantic lies concerning these ancient peoples, neither of them in scripture:

1) The House of Israel became "lost", after it was taken into the Assyrian Captivity in 722 B.C.

2) The House of Judah became a remnant, from which Sephardic Jews are descended and named, after they went into the Babylonian Captivity in 586 B.C.

First of all, the House of Israel, or Northern Kingdom, was not lost at all – except its identity and its name. It is important to know that *God never equated the house of Israel with the house of Judah again in the Old Testament, after these scriptures!*

On the rare times that He spoke of all 12 tribes as a unit again, He called them either the *children of Israel,* or "all Israel." He does promise *a joining together again* in Ezekiel 37, but that will only be in Christ.

So, here is my tentative answer to why God divided them: they were to have two very different destinies. The House of Israel, after it would be taken into the Assyrian Captivity, would lose its identity and its name, but become an enormous number – as the sands of the sea! (Remember the prophecy to Rebecca that she would have *billions* of descendants? And also, the promise to Abraham was that "*in Isaac shall thy seed be called*"!) These prophecies were fulfilled in the Indo-European peoples – a list of which appears in the appendix of this book.

Since everything I have discovered since agrees totally with this summary written for my 1981 book, *Hear, O Israel,* here it is:

"*Webster's Unabridged* listing under "Indo-European languages says this:

'The most important linguistic family of the globe, comprising the chief languages of Europe together with the Indo-Iranian and other Asiatic tongues…also called Indo-Germanic…established their descent from a common ancestor…probably in Eastern Europe…'

"It seems very likely that the *'common ancestor' of all the Indo-European peoples was Abraham.*" However, the countries of Europe seemed reluctant to face their Hebrew origins.

Yet, William Tyndale (1490-1536) first to translate the Hebrew O.T. and Greek N.T. into English, blasted those ideas. He wrote, 'The Greek agreeth more with the English than with the Latyne, and the properties of the Hebrew tongue agreeth a thousand times more with the English than with the Latyne.'" [6]

Whom are you going to believe? The 'neo-cons' of our own day, or William Tyndale, who began life as a skeptic; then met Erasmus at Cambridge and was gloriously saved? He spent the rest of his short life translating the Bible into English; and who was taken into custody in Antwerp, tried in 1536 after 15 months in prison, and burned at the stake as a martyr on 10/6/1536!

God told *where* the Assyrians took the house of Israel in Second Kings 18:9-12 – modern Iraq, and Amos 6:2, Calnah – the east bank of the Tigris River! Is the Word of God up-to-date, or what?

In the 19th century, there were huge discoveries in the field of archeology which unlocked many of the mysteries from the Assyrian empire of 2700 years ago. There was the French consul, Paul E. Botta, stationed at Mosul, Iraq, who began digging and discovered Ninevah under a big 'tell' [i.e. mound of sand] in 1842; then abandoned it in 1843 for Khorasbad in 1843, becoming the first modern man to view the Assyrian ruins.

Then there was the British Austen Henry Layard, who from

boyhood longed to visit Mesopotamia [i.e., Iraq] and see what lay beneath the tells there. He first saw *Birs Nimrud* on 4/16/1840 – the Tower of Babel. Later he spent seven years digging there, un-covering the famous *Nimrod Ivories* on his third day at the site. [7]

During the Christmas holiday of 1845, he met Sir Henry Rawlinson, the foremost Assyriologist and cuneiform expert. He had already been working on the secrets of the Behistun Rock for 10 years, at that point!

The first four years, Rawlinson, a British military officer, made plaster of Paris molds from the bas relief 25 by 50 feet above a ledge 350 feet above the village of Behistun, Iran, on the cliff side of the Zagros Mountains. It was the same message in three lan-guages from King Darius I, to his conquered, peoples – Persians, Babylonians, and Elamites, in about 515 B.C. Since they were an-cient languages, no one had cracked them yet – Old Persian Cu-neiform, Elamite (Susian), and Babylonian cuneiform. Where he could reach, he made the plaster molds from the path at the top of the cliff – from 14 to 18 inches wide at its largest point. Where he could not reach, he worked from a suspended cage. [8]

As he sent his sketches from the plaster molds back to his brother, Sir George Rawlinson, an ancient history professor at Oxford Uni-versity, both were convinced they would eventually decipher them and unlock secrets about where the "Lost Tribes" went when they fled from Iraq. That information was on Column V, a supplemen-tary half-column on the Behistun Rock. It spoke of a revolt " by *Saku'ka*, the chief of the *Sacae*, who dwelt upon the Tigris." He also found that the *Saka Humavaska* in the Persian text corre-sponded to the *Gimirra Umburga* of the Babylonian text. Sir Henry's conclusion was that "We have reasonable grounds for re-garding the *Gimiri,* or Cimmerians, who first appeared in the con-fines of Assyria and Media in the 7th century B.C., and the *Sacae* of the Behistun Rock, nearly two centuries later, as identical with Israel." [9] .

Why? First, there is the obvious fact that the *Sacae* dwelt on the shores of the Tigris River, that northern part of ancient Assyria and modern Iraq where Gozan lay – the place *where the Bible says Israel was taken captive. Second, the term Gimiri has several versions* in ancient manuscripts, ranging from *Ghomri* to *Khumri* to *Humri*. In the British Museum the black "Nimrud Obelisk" of Shalmaneser II has this inscription: "The tribute of *Yahua Abil Khumri,"* or "the tribute of Jehu, son of Khumri." Of this inscription Unger writes, "For a century after Omri's reign the Assyrians were still referring to Israel as 'the land of the House of Omri.' Jehu, a later Israelite usurper, is styled *"Mar Humri'* ('son,', i.e. royal successor of Omri)." [10]

It is well to remember that, after 2500 years of silence on the subject, the Assyrian finds connected the ancient people of the House of Israel with the Saxons of western Europe. Thus, with the phrase God said to Abraham, in commanding him to send away Ishmael (Genesis 21:12) – *"for in Isaac shall thy seed be called"* – we see an amazing affirmation from the Behistun Rock.

As Americans, we think of Isaac as pronounced "I (long I, first syllable stressed)- followed by a non-stressed "saac." Yet Hebrew scholars tell us it is the opposite of the ancient pronunciation of the name, which was a short I, followed by second syllable stress: I-Saac.' As the tribes traveled up into the Caucasus Mountains, and to ancient Caucasia above (in the steppes of Central Asia), they became known as the "sons of Isaac" or the Sons of Saac: the Saxons. (They simply dropped the short "I.") [11]

"Ptolemy mentions a Scythian race sprung from the Sakai, called Saxones; they came, he said, from the country of the Medes. Pliny, a first-century Roman, said, "The Sakai were among the most distinguished people of Scythia who *settled in Armenia* and were called *Sacca-Sani.*" [12]

"Albinus said, 'The Saxons were descended from the ancient Sacae of Asia, and that in process of time they came to be called Saxons.'

"Aeschylus, the celebrated Greek poet, specially mentions that ' The Sacae were noted for good laws, and were preeminently a righteous people.'

"Prideaux says, 'The Cimbrians were driven from the country by a people called Aesaec, who came from between the Euxine and Black Seas, from whom came those Angli, who, with the Saxons, afterwards took possession of England.'

"On the Ninevah Marbles we read that a people called *Esakska* rebelled against the Assyrians about 670 B.C., that is nearly fifty years after the captivity.

"In 516 B.C. Darius Hystapes inscribed on a famous rock called the 'Behistan' the history of 'Iskunka,' the chief of the Sacae who rebelled against him." [13]

Before the Assyrian Captivity, the battle-axe is not mentioned in Scripture as a weapon of Israel, but God says in Jeremiah 51: 20, *"Thou art my battle axe and weapons of war; for with thee will I break in pieces the nations, and with thee will I destroy kingdoms."*

Another clue to the early origin of these people is found in a Danish secular history, based on archeological finds: "The Battle-Axe people in south Scandinavia came from regions with metal objects....The outstanding work of the age are the bronze 'lures'(600 B.C.)." [14]

Now, perhaps the words of the great Anglo-Saxon historian, Sharon Turner (1768-1847), are in order. He devoted his life to the study of manuscripts in the British Museum. "The Anglo-Saxons, Lowland Scotch, Germans, Danes, Norwegians, Swedes, Dutch, Belgians, Lombards, and Franks have all sprung from the great fountain of the human race, which we have distinguished by the term Scythian, German, or Gothic....The first appearance of the Scythian tribes in Europe may be placed, according to Strabo and Homer, about the 8th, or according to Herodotus, in the 7th century before Christ." [15]

My 1981 book, *Hear, O Israel,* traced these people over the centuries into their various homes in Europe. It will be sufficient here to go to Scripture, rather than secular history, to see what the Almighty has told us of their journeyings and destiny.

In Hosea, God gave the prophet this strange command: "*And*

41

the Lord said to Hosea,'Go, take unto thee a wife of whoredoms: for the land hath committed great whoredom, departing from the LORD.' So he went and took Gomer the daughter of Diblaim: which conceived and bare him a son. And the Lord said, 'Call his name Jezreel; for yet a little while, and I will avenge the blood of Jezreel upon the house of Jehu, and will cause to cease the kingdom of the house of Israel. And it shall come to pass that I will break the bow of Israel in the valley of Jezreel. ''' [16]

This message is as clear as a bell. The whoredom of Israel was "departing from the LORD." Jehu was the leader of Israel whom God chose to bring judgment on the whole family of Ahab and Jezebel, but the land of Jezreel was to be avenged of the blood he shed. After that, "the kingdom of the house of Israel" would cease; the Northern Kingdom of Israel would be taken into the Assyrian Captivity, and God would "break the bow of Israel in the valley of Jezreel" – i.e., end its military prowess.

Jezreel was "a city in the territory of Issachar, about 55 miles north of Jerusalem, identified with the modern *Zerin*...In or near the town was a temple of Baal and an asherah (KJV, a grove)" – both places where Israel had gone into spiritual adultery or whoredom, worshipping pagan gods. [17]

Afterward, his wife conceived a daughter, and Hosea was told: " '*Call her name Loruhamah; for I will no more have mercy on the the house of Israel, but I will utterly take them away. But I will have mercy upon the house of Judah, and will save them by the LORD their God, and will not save them by bow, nor by battle, by horses, nor by horsemen.*'" [18]

When Gomer had her third child, God said, " '*Call his name Loammi: for ye are not my people, and I will not be your God. Yet the number of the children of Israel shall be shall be as the sand of the sea, which cannot be measured nor numbered; and it shall come to pass, that in the place where it was said unto them, 'Ye are not my people,' there it shall be said unto them, 'Ye are the sons of the living God.'*

"*Then shall the children of Judah and the children of Israel be gathered together, and appoint themselves one head, and they shall come out of the land: for great shall be the day of Jezreel.*" [19]

Later, in this amazing book, God says, "*Ephraim feedeth on wind, and followeth after the east wind.*" [20] *Ephraim* refers to the whole northern kingdom, the house of Israel here, and this verse tells which way they went. An east wind pushes west, and that is what the house of Israel has been doing ever since. First, the steppes of central Asia, then, western Europe; then England, America and Canada, and then, Australia and New Zealand. During this great migration, the population of the house of Israel would become huge − "as the sand of the sea" and the people would not be known as God's people. But later, in the same areas where they had been called barbarians and Gentiles, "it shall be said unto them, '*Ye are the sons of the living God.*'

This would be much later, when they would hear the gospel of the Lord Jesus, and respond in huge numbers. When Judah and Israel shall come together "*and appoint themselves one head,*" that clearly points to the Lord Jesus Christ, who is the head of the church.

But there is a big clue, in this marvelous book that calls both Israel and Judah to repentance, over and over again: "*Come, and let us return unto the LORD; for He hath torn, and He will heal us; He hath smitten, and He will bind us up. After two days will He revive us: in the third day He will raise us up, and we shall live in His sight. Then shall we know, if we follow on to know the LORD…*" [21]

The phrase "after two days" is the key. I believe that God put the following verse into the Bible for this purpose: "*But beloved, be not ignorant of this one thing, that one day is with the Lord as a thousand years, and a thousand years as one day.*" [22]   If a prophetic "day" is a thousand years, then our recent entrance into the 3rd millennium after the First Advent of the Lord Jesus is significant. Perhaps Almighty God has had enough of people distorting the history of His people Israel, and is planning to revive us, raise us up, and we shall live in his sight.

Maybe God divided the tribes into two kingdoms because of

His eventual plan to bring us together in Christ – which He is surely doing today! But there have always been tremendous differences between Judah and Israel, which have existed from the time of their split to the present time.

In the next chapter, we shall shine our light on Judah, and on the others who call themselves "Jews."

Now, let's look at who the Jews are, in our own day.

CHAPTER 5

Will the Real Jews Please Stand up?

Are the people we recognize as Jews "real Jews"? Are they descendants of the house of Judah – the *Yehudim* of the Hebrew Old Testament? Or, if they cannot meet that test, are they at least *Ioudaioi* – Judeans, as the Greek New Testament referred to them?

If any professing Jews do not meet either of these tests, then they are not the people of the Book. As such, they are not descendant from the tribes, nor do they have any right to a "law of return," since none of their ancestors were ever there in the first place!

The clear answer to these questions is that the remnant of Judah is *known only to Almighty God.* However, there will be at least 12,000 of them on the earth before Christ returns, because Revelation 7:5 says so. Until God humbles them, & brings them to faith in the Lord Jesus Christ, they remain under the curse their ancestors placed on them, when they yelled out to Pilate, *"His blood be on us and on our children."* [1]

No group of Jews opposed the Lord Jesus like the Pharisees. Several times He had big confrontations with them, and He made it very clear that they could not be God's people unless they renounced some of the terrible teaching of their rabbis. He called it their "tradition."

Matthew 23 lists a long list of woes to them because of making themselves God's enemies.

Here are a few of my favorite quotes from that chapter:

"Woe unto you, scribes and Pharisees, hypocrites! For you compass sea and land to make one proselyte, and when he is made, ye make him twofold more the child of hell than yourselves." [v. 15]

"Ye blind guides, which strain at a gnat, and swallow a camel!" [v. 24]

"Woe unto you, scribes and Pharisees, hypocrites! For ye are like unto whited sepulchers, which indeed appear beautiful outward, but are within full of dead men's bones." [25]

"Ye serpents, ye generation of vipers, how can ye escape the damnation of hell?" [v. 33]

"Behold, your house is left unto desolate. For I say unto you, Ye shall not see me henceforth, till ye shall say, Blessed is He that cometh in the name of the Lord." [v. 38 & 39]

Those "traditions of the Pharisees" were just oral in the First Century, however. It took the "dispersion" [the diaspora], between the 2nd and 7th centuries A.D. for the Jews to write down a written series of books which became the authority for Judaism. They called this *The Babylonian Talmud.*

Here are two quotes from top Jewish scholars and Zionists of the 20th century who verified that the authority for Judaism is not the Bible at all, but the *Talmud.*

"…in many matters, Talmudism was a clear departure from Biblical theory and practice…" [2] That is the opinion of the late Claude G. Montifiore, quoted by the late Stephen S. Wise, considered the chief Zionist in America during the last century.

A Jewish writer of a century ago, Arsene Darmesteter, wrote: "Nothing, indeed, can equal the importance of the *Talmud*…It is not understood that it is a human product, whose origin and development are human….

"We no longer have dealings with an inconstant people hesitating between Baal and Jehovah, but with a nation that has made its choice, and enthusiastically accepts and develops a cult….In a word, Hebraism [the Old Testament Scriptures] is at an end; Judaism is born." [3]

What *is* this religion, then – and do we have a commentary on it in the Bible? Yes, it is the religion of the Pharisees, which the Lord Jesus Christ condemned in the firmest possible way. It is vividly referred to in the New Testament passages from the Book of Revelation:

"And unto the angel of the church at Smyrna write: These things saith the first and the last, which was dead, and is alive; I know thy works, and tribulation, and poverty, (but thou art rich) and I know the blasphemy of them which say they are Jews, and are not, but are the synogogue of Satan. Fear none of those things which thou shalt suffer: behold, the devil shall cast some of you into prison, that ye may be tried; and ye shall have tribulation ten days: be thou faithful unto death, and I will give thee a crown of life. He that hath an ear, let him hear what the Spirit saith unto the churches: He that overcometh shall not be hurt of the second death." [4]

"And to the angel of the church in Philadelphia, write; These things saith He that is holy, He that is true, He that hath the key of David, He that openeth and no man shutteth; and shutteth and no man openeth, I know thy works: behold, I have set before thee an open door, and no man can shut it: for thou hast a little strength, and hast kept my word, and hast not denied my name. Behold, I will make them of the synogogue of Satan, which say they are Jews, and are not, but do lie; behold, I will make them to come and worship before thy feet, and to know that I have loved thee. Because thou hast kept the word of my patience, I also will keep thee from the hour of temptation, which shall come upon all the world, to try them that dwell upon the earth.

"Behold, I come quickly: hold that fast which thou hast, that no man take thy crown. Him that overcometh will I make a pillar in the temple of my God, and He will go no more out: and I will

write upon him the name of my God, and the name of the city of my God, which is new Jerusalem, which cometh down out of heaven from my God: and I will write upon Him my new name." [5]

The people who believe and practice the religion of the *Talmud* "say they are Jews, and are not, but are the synogogue of Satan."

It is fascinating that the churches addressed in these verses are warned that they face heavy trials – real suffering, but there is no rebuke for them. In fact, of the messages to the seven churches of Asia Minor that the glorified Christ sends to believers in Smyrna and Philadelphia, there is no rebuke: only encouragement and a promise of great eternal reward as they are steadfast to the end.

However, the "spoiled brat" theology of the Dispensationalists does not like these messages. In their false teaching there is no room for testing or suffering. There is, instead, a Great Escape – the Pre-tribulation Rapture of the saints, which teaches no one to "stand, in the evil day," but only to get ready for the Lift-off! In fact, the series of "Left Behind" books by Tim LaHaye and Jerry Jenkins have reportedly made $43 million for their authors and distributors, in the last decade.

Our friend Ron Poch, another Christian writer and a pastor, has written *I WANT to be Left Behind* to counter this false teaching. We highly recommend it. You may order it from your local Christian bookstore, who will order it from the publisher, Liberty Press in Adrian MI 49221, or write the author directly about what to send to get it from him: Arrows of Truth, P.O. Box 108, Kennesaw, GA 30144.

The Apostle Paul wrote of the great danger in which he found the Galatian believers. Through his preaching they had come to Christ and been gloriously saved – and then were in great spiritual danger because of the Judaizers who were coming behind him, telling them they had to be circumcised and keep the whole Old Testament law! Not only did he rebuke these false teachers. He warned these new believers not to listen to them – to understand that these Judaizers were accursed because of such false teaching.

48

Read the Book of Galatians carefully and prayerfully to understand what a serious issue this is with Almighty God. No one can change the gospel itself without facing divine judgment for such a sin. Salvation is a gift; it can never be earned or deserved.

"For by grace are ye saved, through faith; and that not of yourselves: it is the gift of God: not of works, lest any man should boast." [6]

These phony Jews of our own time on this planet are in terrible danger, as they discard the Bible completely and turn to the *Talmud.*

In that book of theirs, they are allowed to do something so evil that Christians should beware when any Jew makes a vow to them – or even gives testimony to knowing Jesus Christ, unless the fruit of godliness is plainly there in the life. They have something they call the *Kol Nidre* [i.e., all oaths] which they say on Yom Kippur, the Day of Atonement. Here it is:

"All vows,…obligations, oaths, and anathemas, whether called 'konam,' *'konas' or by any other name, which we may vow or swear or pledge, or whereby we may be bound, from this Day of Atonement until the next (whose happy coming we await), we do repent. May they be deemed absolved, annulled, and void, and made of none effect; they shall not bind us nor have power over us. The vows shall not be reckoned vows; the obligations shall not be obligatory, nor the oaths be oaths."* [7]

In stark contrast to this unbelievable excusing of their sin is this verse from the Torah – to us, the Pentateuch:

"When thou shalt vow a vow unto the LORD thy God, thou shalt not slack to pay it: for the LORD thy God will surely require it of thee; and it would be sin in thee." [8]

Who *are* these people, then, if they are not of the tribes; yet are pushing their Zionist agenda in the most evil way that has ever been seen on this planet?

They are of two groups: the Edomites who were living in Judea at the time of Christ, and the Khazars, whose *kagan (king) had them all converted to Judaism at once, in the 8th century B.C.* Of course, these are not the names by which they are known today. The Eastern European Jews are known as Ashkenazic, or Yiddish-speaking Jews, descended from the Khazars.

Benjamin Freedman, of a distinguished Jewish background in New York, became a Catholic with his wife at the age of 25. A strong Christian patriot, he had strong words of warning and advice for U.S. Christians. In 1974 he gave a powerful message to a military organization in Washington, DC.

Freedman said flatly, "The word 'Jew' has been used for a purpose by the people who got us into two world wars, who laid a trap to get us into a third one, and who have practically taken over the control of the world, especially the control of this country....I am certain that, unless something is done to change the thinking of 200 million U.S. Christians, that this country is headed for disaster....You have been told that it is your Christian duty to help repatriate 'God's Chosen People' to their promised land. You have been told that by every media of mass information, including the pulpit, including every other means by which they can shape your thinking....

"Now, I'll tell you what a lie that is! I can cite the sources here that I've consulted, maybe 234 official documents, maps, books, and other records, but the best is one that I found in the last few years, *The Encyclopedia Brittanica, the 1911 Edition, Volume 15,* three pages describe the word 'Khazar'...The Khazars were an Asian nation; they were a Mongoloid, Turko-Finn tribal nation in Asia. And they had so much trouble with the other nations there, who finally succeeded in driving them out of Asia, across the border in what is known today as Russia, in the area of the Ukraine. They found there a lot of peaceful, agricultural people, mostly Slavic, and they conquered them. They did the same thing then as they are still doing in the Middle East! They took them, for no reason at all, except the people weren't trained to fight! They established there the Khazar kingdom." [9]

Next, we see the revelation given to the Father of our country about the destiny of the United States. The 3rd great peril has not happened yet, but it could at any time. We do not have to wait for any enemies to invade.

They are already here.

CHAMBERS OF
JUSTICE SANDRA DAY O'CONNOR

May 19, 1988

Ms. Annetta Conant
6380 E. Shiprock
Apache Junction, AZ 85219

Dear Neta,

You wrote me recently to inquire about any holdings of this Court to the effect that this is a Christian Nation. There are statements to such effect in the following opinions:

Church of the Holy Trinity v. United States,
143 U.S. 457 at 471 (1892);

Zorach v. Clauson,
343 U.S. 306 at 313 (1952);

McGowan v. Maryland,
366 U.S. 420 at 461 (1961).

I enclose a copy of the Church of the Holy Trinity opinion as requested.

With best regards,

Sandra

CHAPTER 6

Washington's Vision at Valley Forge

Today, many refuse to acknowledge that America was founded as a Christian Republic, not a "pluralistic democracy." As usual, the major enemies of that fact are the ones who consider themselves "the Chosen People."

Senator Howard Metzenbaum [D-OH] gave an ominous challenge to this fact in his campaign for re-election in 1988. Addressing a Jewish audience at the Wise Center in Cincinnati, he warned that his hearers "should not allow the forces of evil to make America a Christian nation"!

The major news media and the national Republican Party saw to it that the story was spiked. We read of it in Lawrence Patterson's *Monthly Lesson in Criminal Politics* [11/88] and Don Wildmon's *American Family Association Journal* [12/88].

General Washington's aide, Anthony Sherman, who was with him at Valley Forge in 1777, told Wesley Bradshaw the following account, on July 4, 1859, 82 years later. It was then published in the *National Tribune,* forerunner of *Stars and Stripes.* These are Sherman's words, quoting George Washington:

"One day, I remember it well, the chilly winds whistled through the leafless trees. Though the sky was cloudless and the sun shone brightly, he remained in his quarters nearly all the afternoon alone. When he came out, I noticed that his face was a shade paler than usual, and there seemed to be something on his mind of more than ordinary importance. Returning just after dusk, he dispatched an orderly to the quarters of an officer I mention, who was presently in attendance. After a preliminary conversation of about an hour, Washington, gazing upon his companion with that strange look of dignity which he alone could command, said to the latter:

"I do not know whether it is owing to the anxiety of my mind, or what, but this afternoon, as I was sitting at this table engaged in preparing a dispatch, something seemed to disturb me. Looking up, I beheld standing opposite me, a singularly beautiful female. So astonished was I, for I had given strict orders not to be disturbed, that it was some moments before I found language to inquire into the cause of her presence. A second, a third, and even a fourth time did I repeat my question, but received no answer from my mysterious visitor except a slight raising of her eyes.

"By this time I felt strange sensations spreading through me. I would have risen, but the riveted gaze of the being before me rendered volition impossible. I assayed once more to address her, but my tongue had become useless. Even thought itself had become paralyzed.

- "A new influence, mysterious, potent, irresistible, took possession of me. All I could do was to gaze steadily, vacantly, at my unknown visitant.
- "Gradually, the surrounding atmosphere seemed as though becoming filled with sensations, and luminous. Everything about me seemed to rarefy, the mysterious visitor herself becoming more airy and yet more distinct to my sight than ever before.
- "I now began to feel as one dying, or rather to experience the sensations which I have sometimes imagined accompany dissolution. I did not think, I did not rea-

54

son, I did not move; all were alike impossible. I was only conscious of gazing fixedly, vacantly at my companion.

- "The First Peril: Presently I heard a voice saying, 'Son of the Republic, look and learn,' while at the same time my visitor extended her arm eastwardly. I now beheld a heavy white vapor at some distance, rising fold upon fold. This gradually dissipated, and I looked upon a strange scene. Before me lay spread out in one vast plain all the countries of the world – Europe, Asia, Africa, and America. I saw rolling and tossing between Europe and America the billows of the Atlantic, and between Asia and America lay the Pacific.

- " 'Son of the Republic,' said the same mysterious voice as before, 'Look and learn.' At that moment, I beheld a dark, shadowy being, like an angel, standing, or rather floating in mid-air, between Europe and America. Dipping water out of the ocean in the hollow of each hand, he sprinkled some upon America with his right hand, while with his left hand he cast some on Europe. Immediately a cloud raised from these countries, and joined in mid-ocean. For a while it remained stationary, and then moved slowly westward, until it enveloped America in its murky folds. Sharp flashes of lightning gleamed through it at intervals, and I heard the smothered groans and cries of the American people.

- "A second time the angel dipped water from the ocean, and sprinkled it out as before. The dark cloud was then drawn back to the ocean, in whose heaving billows it sank from view.

- "A third time I heard the mysterious voice saying, 'Son of the Republic, look and learn.' I cast my eyes upon America, and beheld villages and towns and cities springing up, one after another, until the whole land from the Atlantic to the Pacific was dotted with them.

55

Again, I heard the mysterious voice saying, 'Son of the Republic, the end of the century cometh, look and learn.'

- The Second Peril: "At this, the dark shadowy angel turned his face southward, and from Africa I saw an ill-omened spectre approach our land. It flitted slowly over every town and city of the latter. The inhabitants presently set themselves in battle array against each other. As I continued looking, I saw a bright angel, on whose brow rested a crown of light, on which was traced the word 'Union,' bearing the American flag, which he placed between the divided nation, and said, 'Remember, ye are brethren.'

- "Instantly, the inhabitants, casting away their weapons, became friends once more, and united around the National Standard.

- The Third Peril: "And again I heard the mysterious voice saying, 'Son of the Republic, look and learn.' At this the dark, shadowy angel placed a trumpet to his mouth, and blew three distinct blasts; he sprinkled it upon Europe, Asia, and Africa.

- "Then my eyes beheld a fearful scene: from each of these countries arose thick, black clouds that were soon joined into one. And throughout this mass there gleamed a dark, red light by which I saw hordes of armed men, who, moving by with the cloud, marched by land and sailed by sea to America, which country was enveloped in the volume of the cloud. And I dimly saw these vast armies devastate the whole country, and burn the villages, towns, and cities that I beheld springing up. As my ears listened to the thundering of the cannon, clashing of swords, and the shouts and cries of millions in mortal combat, I heard again the mysterious voice saying, 'Son of the Republic, look and learn.' When the voice had ceased, the dark, shadowy angel placed his trumpet once more to his mouth, and blew a long and fearful blast.

■ "Instantly a light as of a thousand suns shone down from above me, and pierced and broke into fragments the dark cloud which enveloped America. At the same moment, the angel upon whose head still shone the word 'Union,' and who bore our national flag in one hand and a sword in the other, descended from the heavens attended by legions of white spirits. These immediately joined the inhabitants of America, who I perceive were well nigh overcome, but who immediately taking courage again, closed up their broken ranks and renewed the battle.

■ "Again, amid the fearful noise of the conflict, I heard the mysterious voice saying,

'Son of the Republic, look and learn.' As the voice ceased, the shadowy angel for the last time dipped water from the ocean and sprinkled it upon America.

"Instantly, the dark clouds rolled back, together with the armies it had brought, leaving the inhabitants of the land victorious.

"Then once more I beheld the villages, towns, and cities springing up where I had seen them before, while the bright angel, planting the azure standard he had brought in the midst of them, cried with a loud voice: 'While the stars remain, and the heavens send down dew upon the earth, so long shall the union last.' And taking from his brow the crown on which was blazoned the word 'Union,' he placed it upon the standard while the people, kneeling down, said, 'Amen.'

"The scene instantly began to fade and dissolve, and I at last saw nothing but the rising, curling vapor I at first beheld. This also disappearing, I found myself gazing once more gazing upon the mysterious visitor, who, in the same voice I had heard before, said:

" 'Son of the Republic, what you have seen is thus interpreted: Three great perils will come upon the Republic. The most fearful is the third, passing which the whole world united shall not prevail against her. Let every child of the Republic learn to live for his God, his land, and Union.'

"With these words the vision vanished, and I started from my seat and felt that I had seen a vision wherein had been shown to me the birth, progress, and destiny of the United States." [1]

The test of a true prophet, says Jeremiah 28:9, is that what he says comes to pass. The first two crises that Washington saw, the War for Independence and the Civil War, were exactly as shown to him. Shall we not expect the Third Peril to be just as accurate?

Furthermore, the "visitant" called Washington "Son of the Republic" — a decade before the *Constitution* was written which gave us our Republic! (Washington accurately called the two males in the vision angels, for he realized there are no female angels in the whole Bible. That is a degree of Bible knowledge not one in a million would have today.)

The first two crises Washington saw have passed: What of the third? Are there "thick, black clouds" through which gleam "a dark, red light" today?

Let us examine the evidence.

As these days move on, we are well into the third millennium and 21st century since the first coming of our Lord Jesus Christ.

During the entire last century there was a great rise of the Red Revolution: the Leftist menace of the 20th century, which saw over half the world enslaved under Communism.

Through the vision and courage of our great Christian President, Ronald Reagan, who had the courage to call the Soviet Union "the evil empire," only China and Cuba still try to keep the Red Revolution alive today. But there is still the ominous promise of the second horse of the Apocolypse:

And when he had opened the second seal, I heard the second beast say, 'Come and see.'

And there went out another horse that was red: and power was given to him that sat thereon to take peace from the earth, and that they should kill one another: and there was given unto him a great sword." [2]

The more we study the above two verses, the less we believe that the Red menace is gone for good. For although World War I killed millions, and World War II multiplied more millions killed, peace has not yet been taken from the whole earth. Ever since 9/11/01, the world has been distracted by the terrorism of radical Islam. Is this a part of the Red Menace taking peace from the earth? Does God's Word have anything to say about the Red Revolution that can give us light on this subject?

Indeed it does! Remember when Esau was hungry, and sold his birthright to Jacob for some red, lentil stew? That was the first time that God said, *"Esau is Edom."* [i.e., red]

The birthright gave the recipient of it a special relationship with the Almighty. God did not take it lightly when man thought nothing of it. In fact, one of the saddest passages in the New Testament is this one: *"Lest there be any fornicator, or profane person, as Esau, who for one morsel of meat, sold his birthright. For ye know how that afterward, when he would have inherited the blessing, he was rejected: for he found no place of repentance, though he sought it carefully with tears"* [3]

It began a blood feud that lasted over the ages – not just in Jacob and Esau, but their descendants. Almighty God lets us know His anger about it, in no uncertain terms. The whole book of Obadiah deals with God's fury against Esau, and His certain judgments against that nation. Several times in scripture God says, "Esau is Edom" – (i.e., Red). But in Malachi He reveals "the bottom line."

"The burden of the word of the LORD to Israel by Malachi. 'I have loved you,' saith the LORD. Yet ye say, 'Wherein hast thou loved us? Was not Esau Jacob's brother?' saith the LORD: ' yet I loved Jacob, and I hated Esau, and laid his mountains and his heritage waste for the dragons of the wilderness.'

"Whereas Edom saith, 'We are impoverished, but we will return and build the desolate places'; thus saith the LORD of hosts, 'They shall build, but I will throw down; and they shall call them The border of wickedness, and, The people against whom the LORD hath indignation forever." [4]

59

Now let us take a long, hard look at that word "Red." No spiritual value or privilege meant anything to Esau when he was hungry. Like the Red revolutionary movement over the ages, the *only issues* that mattered were the economic ones – including the filling of one's stomach and the gratifying of physical desires of all kinds.

In the New Testament, the Almighty said, *"As it is written, Jacob have I loved, but Esau have I hated."* [5]

Now, remember that in the Old Testament, *Yehudim* meant of the tribe of Judah, but by New Testament times, the Greek word *Ioudaiois* meant simply "a Judean." That is because of the following facts:

"...in the days of John Hyrcanus [end of 2nd century B.C. – Ed.]...the Edomites became a section of the Jewish people." [6]

"They were then incorporated with the Jewish nation..."[7]

"...from then on they constituted a part of the Jewish people, Herod being one of their descendants." [8]

"...they were hereafter no other than Jews." [9]

Perhaps that is why God prepared a message *cut in stone, on the Behistun Rock, to identify his "lost" House of Israel as Saxons!* Once this land was filled with enemies, designed to destroy this republic, the true Christians would need an authoritative word about *who they are* to inspire them to fight a seemingly hopeless battle.

We have examined what God's true Israel is. Now let us look at *What America is, to God Almighty.*

In the providence of God, an amazing manuscript was mailed to us over 25 years ago. Its author was Dr. Charles W. Ewing, and he sent it shortly before he died. It confirmed to me that no other nation but America has had its beginnings so rooted in a covenant relationship with God. It convinced me that the nation born at Sinai has been reborn here. That is why attempts to turn it into a humanistic, socialist state are so serious. The powers of darkness simply cannot stake a permanent claim to this land.

Dr. Ewing wrote, "We were all taught in school that this great continent was named after the geographer, Amerigo Vespuci, but we were not taught the meaning of this man's first name.

60

"Professor Miskovsky, scientist in Etymology at Oberlin College, Oberlin, Ohio, brought out some astonishing facts about the word 'America.' The Latin form of Amerigo is 'Americus,' and the feminine form of 'Americus' is 'America.'

"The old Gothic form (keep in mind that the Goths were Israelites) for the word 'America' was *Amel Ric. Amel Ric* is still found in the German language in a slightly corrupted form as *Emerich....Amel* means 'heaven' and *Ric* means 'kingdom.' Together the two words mean 'Kingdom of Heaven.'" [10]

How are we going to restore what God gave us, here?

"*If the foundations be destroyed, what can the righteous do?*" [11]

There is only one answer. *RESTORE THE FOUNDATIONS!* It will require more prayer, more claiming of the promises of God's Word, and more faith than you and I have ever exercised before. But the vision God gave the Father of our Country should encourage us to do it!

Did any of our Founding Fathers foresee this as a possible threat? How about this warning in 1778 from George Washington, himself?

"It is much to be lamented, that each State, long ere this, has not hunted them [the Jews] down, as pests to society, and the greatest enemies we have to the happiness of America...No punishment, in my opinion, is too great for the man who can build his greatness on his country's ruin." [12]

On the first Sunday of the new year in 1960, my husband and I heard a prophetic message from our pastor, Rev. Leroy Webber, at Long Hill Chapel in Chatham, New Jersey. He said we were entering an age when the only virtue would be "tolerance." Christians would be persecuted for pointing out sins or any evils contrary to God's Word. Criticism of any religions or occult philosophies that deny Christianity would be forbidden. The only religion which could be criticized with impunity would be *the Christian faith!*

The message made a terrific impression on us. We were never

able to forget it. Now, what he predicted is the great reality. "Christian-bashing" is the only allowed intolerance of our time.

Recently, Dr. D. James Kennedy spoke on the same subject on his radio program, "Truths that Transform." But he said that the definition of tolerance is far different today than what we have believed all our lifetimes. *Webster's New World Dictionary* says of tolerance: " being tolerant, esp. of views, beliefs, practices etc. of others that differ from one's own."

Dr. Kennedy insisted that what is meant by tolerance *now* is *accepting other views and lifestyles as equally vaid with your own!* Thus, we are warned. The days of beheading for disagreement with antichrist principles may not be far away. In fact, the recent beheadings in Iraq may indicate the time is already here!

See Revelation 20:4 for such a time, prophesied in Holy Writ.

CHAPTER 7

The Red Revolution & Mark of the Beast

The biggest delusion under which most Christians in America operate is the notion that we share the Old Testament with Jews as the basis of our faith.

We have already shown that modern Jews use *The Talmud* to justify their wickedness. A quotation from my book, *A Call to War,* should help the reader to understand:

In the 1970's an author named Betty Esses DeBlase wrote a book exposing her ex-husband, Michael Esses. "She tells a sickening tale of lies and duplicity by her ex-husband; even that he made up the story of the Lord Jesus appearing to him in a vision, which he wrote about in a popular book, *Michael, Michael, Why Do You Hate Me?*"

"During the 1970's a personal friend of our family was a student at the Melodyland School of Theology in Anaheim, California, when Esses taught there.

"He was concerned about the tragic events that kept happening to the Esses, especially the loss of their small son when their house burned down. As he prayed and fasted for them, the Lord impressed upon him that Satan's ground in Esses' life was his clinging to *The Talmud.*

"Visiting Esses, our friend asked him if he still owned the *Talmud.* When he said 'yes,' the student confronted him with the fact that it contained sorcery and condoned perversions such as pederasty. However, most serious of all are its blasphemies against our Lord Jesus Christ.

"The confronted Esses flew into a rage, saying he would never get rid of the *Talmud,* his 'holy book.'" [1]

It is high time Christians understand that the *Talmud,* on which most modern Jewish beliefs are based, is not biblical at all. It is *cabalistic….*Basically, it is a system of ancient Hebrew sorcery which features magic rites being derived from the numerical combinations of Old Testament Scriptures! In other words, the cabalist cares nothing for what God says: only that he believes occult rites are hidden there.

Since cabalism is the source of the Red, revolutionary movement, we are going to give a brief summary of that beast system from my book, *Return of the Puritans,* here:

"Most people think socialism was born in the 19th century in the mind of Karl Marx….Early in the 20th century a Christian historian in England, Nesta Webster, made a vast study of the occult-based world revolutionary movement. Her work has never been refuted…. She traces the source of modern socialism back to the ancient, magical cabala (or Kabbalah) of the Hebrews…[where] 'the theosophical doctrines of Israel are to be found.' These were finally written down in two books: the *Sepher Yetzirah* and the *Zohar,* and are confirmed by the Babylonian *Talmud.*" [2]

"However, to accept the occult Cabala amounts to a total denial of the Bible…Nesta Webster summarizes the devastating effects of the evil Cabalistic teachings as follows:

'Perversion is the keynote of all the debased forms of Gnosticism. According to Eliphas Levi, certain of the Gnostics introduced into their rites that profanation of Christian mysteries which was to form the basis of black magic in the Middle Ages…The Gnostics, says Eliphas Levi, under the pretext of spiritualizing matter, materialized the spirit in the most revolting ways...Rebels to the hierarchic order...they wished to substitute the mystical license of sensual passion to wise Christian sobriety and obedience to laws...Enemies of the family, they wished to produce sterility by increasing debauchery.'" [3]

"Webster traces the sinister tradition to 9th-century Islam, subverted by a Gnostic Dualist, Abdullah ibn Maymun...initiating only a small number of his own type into the secrets of the sect....nine French gentlemen bound themselves into an order for the protection of pilgrims to the Holy Sepulchre in Jerusalem in 1118....They became known as the Knights Templar, sanctioned by the Council of Troyes and the Pope in 1128 to be an order of poverty, chastity, and obedience. However, they amassed a fortune in alms and reparations, and spread all over Europe by the end of the 12th century.

"During the 13th century, the Knights Templar became known for rapacity, drunkenness, aggrandizement, and lack of scruples...All groups of Templars confessed to denying Christ and spitting on a crucifix as part of their initiation rites. Modern Satanist cults also engage in such practices....Templar heresies were...the Unitarian deism of Islam." [4]

The rest of the Middle Ages saw the birth and growth of Illuminism and Freemasontry, which culminated in 1776 with the founding of the *Illuminati* by Adam Weishaupt on May 1 — truly a Mayday for the whole world, launching "his scheme for the destruction of all religion and existing governments." [5] A Jew who had been educated by the Jesuits, he advocated a system of neoplatonism, featuring a three-class society made up of ruling, military, and working people. [6]

All of the main leaders of the *Illuminati* were apostates. "Weishaupt was assisted in his scheme by a Baron Adolf Knigge, who helped him unite radical Masonic lodges in Germany toward a goal of world government...Other important *Illluminati* were Count Mirabeau (a prime force in the French Revolution), a foe of religion named Nicholai, and a lawyer named Zwack." [7]

An ill-fated ex-evangelical named Lanze was carrying documents for the group when he was hit by lightning on horseback en route to Silesia in July of 1785. Information found by police on his corpse ended the secrecy of the cult, and the Bavarian government suppressed it in 1786. [8]

Weishaupt died in Germany in 1830, but by then had finantical followers Marx and Engels spreading his poison.

Karl Marx was also an apostate Jew.

Do you still doubt what the "Synogogue of Satan" is? If it is still hard for you to believe, please read the following scripture and compare it with comments on the *Talmud,* from reputable Jewish sources in notes below.

Like many of you, I grew up in a home where "one's word was his bond." To break your word was the worst of all sins. How then does this verse judge the *Kol Nidre* practice of the Jews? *"If a man vow a vow unto the LORD, or swear an oath to bind his soul with a bond, he shall not break his word; he shall do according to all that proceedeth out of his mouth."* (9)

The teachings of the *Talmud* are so vile that I simply refuse to quote any of them – particularly the blasphemous passages about our Lord and Savior, Jesus Christ, and his mother. For those who want more documentation, here is a good source of quotes from the *Talmud.* It is by a Roman Catholic priest, I. B. Pranaitis, entitled *The Talmud Unmasked.* It is a small paperback available for $10 postpaid, from Emissary Publications, 9205 S.E. Clackamas Road, Clackamas, OR 97015. The quotes endorse and advocate pedophilia, homosexuality, and other perversions, revealing plainly a Judaism that has cut all ties to the *Torah* and Old Testament scriptures and to the Holy One of Israel. Judaism is Talmudism, not the religion of the Old Testament. Therefore, those Christians who insist on using the term "Judeo-Christian" need to be aware of the complete oxymoron that term is – on the level of "satanic-Christian" or some such term.

It is because of the grief that term brings to me every time I hear it, deep in my spirit, that I am writing this book. This author truly believes that the blessed Holy Spirit will not tolerate this ignorance much longer. Remember, in the Old Testament even the "sins of ignorance" had to be atoned for. If this is the first warning the reader has received on this dangerous practice, he is urged to repent at once, never to repeat the term again. *"For if we sin willfully, after that we have received the knowledge of the truth, there remaineth no more sacrifice for sins."* [10]

The term 'Israel,' as indicated earlier, was to define a people who prevailed with God and man. The New Testament clearly limits the term to *believers* in the Lord Jesus Christ, regardless of ethnic background. *"Now to Abraham and his seed were the promises made. He saith not, and to seeds, as of many, but as of one, and to thy seed, which is Christ."* [11]

"There is neither Jew nor Greek, there is neither bond nor free, there is neither male nor female: for ye are all one in Christ Jesus. And if ye be Christ's, then are ye Abraham's seed, and heirs according to the promise." [12]

All the land promises of God to ancient Israel were fulfilled with the return of a remnant of Judah and a few from other tribes from the Babylonian Captivity to Jerusalem. The biblical books of Ezra, Nehemiah, Haggai, and Zechariah, cover this period. The purpose of their return to the Holy Land was to rebuild the temple, and the wall around Jerusalem itself − to keep the messianic line pure for the Incarnation of the Lord Jesus.

It is indeed fascinating that it was the Khazars − those with no Israelite blood in them, descendant from a Turko-Finnish, non-Semitic stock − who conspired to get a stranglehold on Palestine, and had the gall to call it "Israel" when they finally got the UN to recognize it in 1948! The duplicity which characterized the Balfour Declaration of 1917 guaranteed the nightmare the Middle East has become in the years since. Here it is:

"His majesty's government view with favor the establishment in Palestine of a national home for the Jewish people and will use their best endeavors to facilitate the achievement of this object, it being clearly understood that nothing shall be done which may prejudice civil and religious rights of existing non-Jewish communities in Palestine, or the rights and political status enjoyed by Jews in any other country." [13]

The British looked on it as the right for Jews to emigrate, buy land, and start businesses; the Jews saw it as the chance to have a state of their own, in the very place where God promised a homeland for Abraham and the original tribes.

On June 16,1918, Commander D.G. Hogarth assured seven exiled Arab leaders living in Cairo that "as far as Palestine is concerned, we are determined that no people shall be subjected to another." According to Hogarth, Sharif "Hussein was willing to welcome Jews to all Arab lands, but would not accept an independent Jewish state." [14]

There was never adequate discussion on who and how many Arabs in Palestine there were. Alfred Lilienthal, author of *The Zionist Connection,* said the British "hoped to conceal the fact that 93 percent of the population was then Christian or Muslim Arab and but 7 percent Jewish....It is hard to find a document that has wrought more tragedy to the world than the Balfour Declaration." [15]

By 1939 the real intent of the Zionists was obvious to all. Eastern European Jews were flooding Palestine. The British tried to calm the situation by issuing the MacDonald White Paper, describing their goal as an independent Palestine within 10 years, which "Arabs and Jews could share in such a way as to ensure that the essential interests of each are safeguarded." [16] Then the British promised an admission of 75,000 more Jews over the next five years, with no immigration thereafter,"unless the Arabs of Palestine are prepared to acquiesce in it." [17]

All hell immediately broke loose. Demonstrations and violence took over, and a British constable was killed. David Ben-Gurion said (8/29/39), "For us the White Paper neither exists nor can exist. We must believe as if we were the State in Palestine until we actually become that State in Palestine." [18]

Meanwhile, President Roosevelt was being pressured to get the

U.S. involved, and sent Brig. General Patrick Hurley to Palestine, so that he would return and give a report directly to FDR. Hurley revealed the real Zionist goals as follows:

"For its part, the Zionist Organization in Palestine has indicated its commitment to an enlarged program for

a) A Sovereign Jewish state which would embrace Palestine and probably Transjordan;

b) *An eventual transfer of the Arab population from Palestine to Iraq; (italics added)*

c) *Jewish leadership for the whole Middle East in the fields of economic development and control."* [19]

There it is – in black and white. *Now,* does the reader see why the Zionist-controlled Bush administration led us in a preemptive strike in Iraq? It had to do with a lot more than taking out a few scud missiles that had been around since the previous Gulf War!

FDR tried to ignore this information, and attempted to rescue 500,000 misplaced Jews in Europe through getting several nations to pledge to take at least 150,000 Jews each, saying we would do the same. The atheist, non-Semitic Jews would have none of it! It was Palestine and nothing else that they wanted, and they were using the Nazi persecution of Jews to raise money from American Jews to get it. All the Jewish lobbyists went to work on Congress, and by December 1942 got 63 senators and 181 House members to issue a joint statement which called on FDR "to restore the Jewish homeland." [20]

Soon the President was reelected for a 4th term, just a few months before the Malta conference. After the Summit meeting between FDR, Churchill, and Stalin, both the American and British leaders were to have meetings with Ibn Saud. "The President is reported to have remarked that he had learned more about the Arab /Jewish situation from Ibn Saud in five minutes than he had understood all his life." [21]

When FDR returned to America, the relentless Zionist pressure on him continued. Although the official cause of his death on

4/12/45 was listed as illness, a shot rang out from his room in Warm Springs, Georgia, a few minutes before the announcement was made. [My late grandfather was told this by phone the very day FDR died, for he knew a worker at the Georgia estate where the president died.] In the months following, many different people mentioned the shot, but the American media covered up the facts immediately, as if it never happened. Speculation will probably never end about whether the real cause was suicide or homicide. However, there was no open viewing; only the flag-draped casket was ever seen.

For years this author wondered why Roosevelt had a former haberdasher for his vice-president. That mystery was solved when we learned that Truman's partner in the business was Jewish. He asked if he could have access to the president whenever he wanted. His wish was granted – with the result that he hounded Truman mercilessly about recognizing Israel as soon as their case was made at the U.N. So the United States became the first nation to recognize Israel – and the rest, as they say, is history.

Ben Hecht's *Perfidy* and Rabbi Moshe Schonfeld's book, *The Holocaust Victims* revealed the extent to which the Zionists went to insure they would get Israel. Ben Hecht exposed "Israeli official Rudolf Kastner of collaboration in the responsibility for the slaughter of Hungary's one million Jews." [22] Schonfeld quoted Jewish Agency Chairman Yitzhak Greenbaum as having said, "One cow in Palestine is worth more than all the Jews in Poland." [23]

However, to a Bible-believing Christian, the most appalling fact about the outlaw Israeli state is the total support for it from America's dispensationalists, who believe the Jews are Israel – even the Khazars, who have no claim whatever to the promises of God to ancient Israel and Judah. (In all fairness, these folks usually know nothing about the Khazars – and do not want any facts replacing their ignorance!)

The Dispensationalists have interpreted *I also will keep thee from the hour of temptation* to mean "the rapture" or miraculous catching away from the earth just before the trouble hits. As I mentioned earlier, this is false teaching, and just what the natural, unregenerate heart of man would like to think. Is it worth it to hang onto this myth, and find yourself one of those who will hear those terrible words from the Lord Jesus Christ at the Judgment? *"Not everyone that saith unto me, 'Lord, Lord,' shall enter into the kingdom of heaven, but he that doeth the will of my father which is in heaven. Many will say unto me in that day, 'Lord, Lord, have we not prophesied in thy name? And in thy name have cast out devils? And in thy name done many wonderful works?'*

"And then will I profess unto them, 'I never knew you: depart from me, ye that work iniquity." [24]

You who fear you are *now* hearing false teaching, get a copy of *I WANT To Be Left Behind,* by Ron Poch. By the way, the scripture he used on the title page of his book was Isaiah 4:3. *"And it shall come to pass, that he that is left in Zion, and he that remaineth in Jerusalem, shall be called holy."* (Read the Book of Zechariah to see that two-thirds of the Jews in Israel will be destroyed in a war, leaving only the one-third whom God calls holy.)

Martin Luther understood what it really meant *to have the fear of God, and not the "fear of the Jews."* Luther fearlessly opposed them for years. An American ministry authorized the translation from the German into a booklet they published, *The Jews & Their Lies.* Luther exposed Jewish chicanery for decades, and preached against them in his last sermon before he died in February of 1546. Here is a quote from it:

"Besides, you also have many Jews living in the country, who do much harm… You should know that the Jews blaspheme and violate the name of our Savior day for day…for that reason you, Milords and men of authority, should not tolerate but expel them. They are our public enemies and incessantly blaspheme our Lord Jesus Christ; they call our Blessed Virgin Mary a harlot and her Holy Son a bastard, and to us they give the epithet of changelings and abortions. If they could kill us all, they would gladly do so; in fact, many of them murder Christians, especially those professing to be surgeons and doctors…

"Therefore, deal with them harshly as they do nothing but excruciatingly blaspheme our Lord Jesus Christ, trying to rob us of our lives, our health, our honour and belongings...For that reason I cannot have patience nor carry on an intercourse with these deliberate blasphemers of our Beloved Saviour." [25]

God is asking you and me to have courage: one rare virtue that few have in our country where the "fear of the Jews" reigns. Remember, "The fear of man bringeth a snare: but whoso putteth his trust in the Lord shall be safe." [26]

In a culture where the so-called Jews have gained control of much of the financial oligarchy, all of the media and the "entertainment industry", the pornography industry, and is actively promoting homosexuality and pederasty, (all things excused and welcomed in the *Talmud) – can you still say with honesty, "Where is all this coming from?" But when policy makers in our government are deliberately sacrificing American lives to benefit the Israeli state, and to provide a place where they can send expelled Palestinians – have they not gone too far?*

By now we are sure that you know this is all about money, as far as the Jews are concerned. It is high time — really, several decades overdue — that we put the Zionists on a diet. How about our writing the politicians to tell them that we see no reason at all for the "neo-cons" or Israeli backers to be getting money for the Israeli state from us any more. I also think it will be wise if we say that we don't plan to vote for politicians who vote for money for them , either. But let's be reasonable.

We could suggest cutting it off a quarter of the amount each year! That way, it would take four years to be out from under that burden. If we are told "no," let's ask, "Why not?"

What are they afraid of? Sometimes it seems as if they hold every one of our politicians in Washington under some kind of blackmail. Perhaps it is nuclear blackmail!

Des Griffin wrote a wonderful article for his *Midnight Messenger*, which was reprinted by MEDIABYPASS.COM in April of 2003, called "The Phony War on Terrorism." It is a superb summary of our current world. He told how Leon Trotsky [i.e. Bronstein] arrived in New York 1/13/1917 and trained what Winston Churchill called "a band of extraordinary personalities" at a Standard Oil facility in New Jersey. In early April 1917, the Trotsky gang left New York aboard the *S.S. Kristianiaford* bound for Petrograd to foment the Bolshevik Revolution. They were funded by $20 million from Jacob Schiff, a Rothschild agent who controlled Kuhn, Loeb & Company in New York. President Wilson provided Trotsky with an American passport to return to Russia and 'carry forward' the revolution.' It opened the way for Trotsky and Lenin to lead the Bolsheviks in their takeover of Russia. [This was the action for which the Khazars had been waiting for 1,000 years!]

This action made "The Balfour Declaration" possible, and two decades later the "perpetration of numerous horrific terrorist acts by Zionists in British-ruled Palestine." The terrorists declared the existence of the "State of Israel" in May of 1948, and massacred 254 women, old men, and children in the Arab town of Deir Yassin — throwing their bodies into a well. Hundreds of thousands of Palestinians fled the country.

Zionist author Jon Kimche called the incident "the darkest stain on the Jewish record throughout the fighting", and said, "The terrorist justified the massacre of Deir Yassin because it led to the panic flight of the remaining Arabs in the Jewish state area.." [27]

That was 56 years ago. Last year, Des Griffin reported the following:

"Israel's Hebrew language radio station Kol Yisrael *recently taped* a discussion between Shimon Peres and Israel's prime minister, Ariel Sharon. In their conversation, Perez urges the prime minister to at least maintain the pretense of trying to end the violence in the Middle East to appease the Ameicans. Enraged, Sharon screamed at Perez, 'Every time we do something, you warn me that America will do this, or America will do that. I will tell you something very clearly: don't worry about American pressure on Israel. We, the Jewish people, control America, and the Americans know it!'" [28]

The Red Jews are planning a world government (both Edomites and Eastern European Khazars) – and they plan to run it! What George Washington saw in the third great peril will soon be upon us. That is why they no longer try to hide their hatred for our Savior and His people. The days of the mark of the beast and the number of his name are not far away. The ACLU, the ADL, and related ilk are determined to wipe out Christianity in our beloved land.

Read *The Six-Pointed Star*, by Dr. O.J Graham, or *Descent into Slavery*, by Des Griffin, and see for yourself. The authors make it clear that the red shield on the door of Mayer Amchel Bauer had that hexagram on it. He changed his name to Rothschild [i..e., Red Shield] of the infamous banking family he started at the end of the 18th century. Graham is a former Jew who had a very real conversion to Christ, and says this evil, witchraft symbol is the *mark of the beast*, and the 666 or six points of the two triangles of it show "the number of his name." Now hear the "prophecy" of Ben Gurion as it appeared in *Look Magazine* in 1962:

"The image of the world in 1987 as traced in my imagination: The Cold War will be a thing of the past. Internal pressure of the constantly growing intelligentsia in Russia for more freedom and the pressure of the masses for raising their living standards may lead to a gradual democratization of the Soviet Union. On the other hand, the increasing influence of the workers and farmers, and the rising political importance of men of science, may transform the United States into a welfare state with a planned economy. Western and Eastern Europe will become a federation of autonomous states having a Socialist and democratic regime.

"*With the exception of the USSR as a federated Eurasian state, all other continents will become united in a world alliance, at whose disposal will be an international police force. All armies will be abolished, and there will be no more wars.* In Jerusalem, the United Nations (a truly UNITED Nations) will build a Shrine of the Prophets to serve the federated union of all continents; this will be the seat of the Supreme Court of Mankind, to settle all controversies

74

among the federated continents…"

How many know that America gives more money to the Israeli state – every year – than any other nation on earth? "But the cost is high: $10 billion a year in taxpayers' money – including interest on money the U.S. *borrows* to give to Israel – and worldwide anger that the U.S. supports the occupation of Palestinian lands." [29]

After giving years of thought to this matter, and asking God how to broach it with typical American Christians, I believe there is an answer. Let me give a hypothetical example.

Let us suppose an unpopular group in our country (say, the illegal aliens) were to have built whole communities where they could live, and not have to worry about learning English or getting along with the majority population. One day, a bunch of men with bull dozers would enter the area and begin demolishing homes.

In America, would it be likely that a second day of this policy would be permitted?

Now, have *you* faced the fact that that *the Israeli state has been doing this on many days in every year* since it was recognized by the United Nations? Yet the Palestinian people are always told, as each of U.S. presidents are by the Israelis, "We must defend ourselves."

Actually, my example is not a very good one. The Palestinians did not come into the land recently, and build their houses. One son of ours had a Palestinian friend in college whose family had owned their home in Bethlehem for 3600 years! They fled in 1948 and came to this country because they were Christians and wanted to be able to practice their faith without interference.

Then, in the name of common sense, how on earth can it happen in Israel – to thousands of Palestinian homes? And in case you are one who has been influenced by Dispensational lies, and told me or others, "Well, God commanded His chosen people to destroy the heathen in Canaan after the Exodus," let us tell you something. Back in the early 1980's my husband and I heard Queen Noor (American widow of the late King Hussein) on a radio program state that *at least 20 percent of the Palestinian people are*

Christians! Do you dare to try to compare them to the pagan heathen whom God allowed over 400 years to repent, before giving the orders to *ancient Israel (i.e., the tribes) to destroy them?*

Anyone who faces what has been going on in Israel since 1948 will agree that it is the biggest example of a tail wagging the dog that the world has ever seen. The obedient dog has been the United States, and its tail is obviously the Israeli state. But when the facts are faced that *Israel could not even exist except for the $10 billion she gets from the U.S. every year,* it becomes much more sinister. [29] (Some sources insist that the amount is far higher than that — possibly as much as over $40 billion a year, with the loan guarantees.)

Now we return to the lies which have been freely circulated as if they were truth by the misguided Dispensationalists of America. Remember the two we mentioned in the fourth chapter? Well, there is another which we have saved for this chapter. It is what the *source of current Jewish belief is: is it the Torah, the Old Testament scriptures, as most naïve Bible-believing Christians believe — or The Talmud?*

The "father of our *Constitution*," James Madison, and member of the House of Representatives in our first Congress, led the First Amendment through the three months of controversy which resulted in its final acceptance. None of the other nine amendments which make up our *"Bill of Rights"* took nearly as much time as this one. Here it is:

"Congress shall make no law respecting an establishment of religion, *or prohibiting the free exercise thereof;* or abridging the freedom of speech, or of the press; or the right of the people peaceably to assemble, and to petition the Government for a redress of grievances."

Please note the italicized phrase, for that was done for a specific purpose, here. It is the most attacked part of our *Constitution,* commonly given the name of "a wall of separation between church and state" by folks bringing their lawsuits to court. You will notice that none of the words of that phrase appear either there or in the earlier clause that precedes it. The phrase *has never been* in our *Constitution!*

Where did it come from, then?

Actually, our 3rd president, Thomas Jefferson, coined the term in his letter to the Danbury Baptists in 1802. He was simply reassuring them that they *could* practice their religion according to their own beliefs, and not be pressured by the larger denomination of Connecticut − probably the Puritans, as was the case of neighboring Massachusetts − known in that time as *"the Bible state."*

It is important to remember that what the colonists feared was a "state church," which was true in England (the Church of England) and in Germany (the Lutheran Church). The "Establishment Clause" was designed to keep any one *denomination* from controlling Christianity in America, or having government approval to do such a thing.

Today, it is obvious that radical, "Red" Jews are behind most of the anti-Christ attacks on the church in America. Just look at the makeup of the early (and current) ACLU − which Dr. Kennedy calls the "Anti-Christian Liberty Union.," and the membership of the founders of the Communist Party in America. (Look them up for yourself, at the reference desk of your local library!)

Now you know. Some of you may be sorry you read this book, thinking God would be less likely to judge you for your apathy and indifference beforehand, if you never learned these things. Forget it! Remember, in the Old Testament even the sins of ignorance had to be atoned for!

Now, you may be realizing what your real problem is. You don't know God's Word well enough to actually know what's right or wrong, a good bit of the time. I will be eternally grateful for Ulric Jelinek, a Christian friend from our church in New Jersey, who challenged me (a year after I became a Christian) as follows:

"Pat, if you really want God to use you in your lifetime, make much of Him and His Word − and He will teach you. Read it through once a year, and get to know it well."

That was excellent advice which has served me well, so I gladly pass it on to you. To accomplish this, think of the Bible as food for your spirit. So plan to "eat" three or four chapters every day, with one memory verse written in a journal as a daily, spiritual "vitamin pill." (The method Dick and I have used for the last 40 years is in my book, *Healing of the Mind.*) It is amazing what happens with verses faithfully learned! I imagine a conveyor belt in my mind that seems to bring these up when I listen to a message, biblical or political, with false teaching in it. I don't get angry or temperamental about it; God's Word just tosses out the error from my mind, and I keep that "peace that passes understanding."

For those of you who are tempted to forget the warnings here, we recommend reading chapter 13 of the Book of Revelation. You will see the awful fate of those who take the "mark of the beast" on their foreheads or right hands.

There is no doubt that we have already lost 95 percent of our freedom in this country. Well, let's use the five percent we still have to try to get the rest back! The showdown is coming, anyway. There is no way we can avoid it. It behooves us in the battle for Truth, for our God, our families, and for this great country He has given us, to counter the lies. I plan to write more congressmen and letters to the editor. Will you join me? Remember, our Lord Jesus said, *"Ye are the salt of the earth: but if the salt has lost his savour, wherewith shall it be salted? It is thenceforth good for nothing, but to be cast out and trodden under foot of men."* [30]

I must have read that a hundred times in our early years in the faith before I suddenly understood it. Why, if we are "trodden under foot of men," we are their slaves!

Salt has some wonderful qualities which the Lord Jesus wants us all to have. First, it makes people thirsty. If our lives are full of his love and wisdom, others may want those qualities, too. Second, it must come in contact with someone to help at all.

One thing is certain, though. Until you join the family of God, you are on the outside, looking in. Everyone is eligible to be saved, to be changed, for "All have sinned and come short of the glory of God." [31] Since no other sinner could have saved us, "God sent

78

His only begotten Son, that whosoever believeth in Him should not perish, but have everlasting life." [32]

You may be thinking, 'how could I qualify? I've blown it so badly – how could the Lord Jesus accept me?" Well, that's why the word gospel means "good news." You don't have to do anything but 1) admit you are a sinner, and 2) repent, and thank Him for dying for *your* sins, and rising from the dead for your justification, and 3) ask Him to come into your life and take over as Lord – i.e., boss.

If you don't really believe yet, then read the gospel of John through until you truly *do believe!*

From then on, just as when you get married, you go out and act like it! That means getting into the Bible every day and spending time with Him in prayer. The better you get to know Him, the more you will want to please Him. It works, every time, if you mean what you say. Soon, the reality of 2 Corinthians 5:17 will be seen in your life: *"Therefore, if any man be in Christ, he is a new creature: old things are passed away; behold, all things are become new."*

Almighty God loves you, and longs to make you into a new person. Bring Him great joy by coming to Him and letting Him make you the person He has always wanted you to be. No one but His own will be able to resist the mark of the beast.

There is nothing ethnic about salvation. Many western peoples will be in heaven; many will not. Some Jews will surely be there, but many will not. Some Africans and Asians will be there, but some will not. It is a *heart matter.* Whoever you are, "harden not your heart" toward Him who is your only hope for eternal life.

It has been my great joy to lead several Jews to Christ. My best friend in high school was a Jew. I have prayed for Doris and her family, who moved to Israel decades ago, that they will come to know the Lord Jesus. (I was not a true Christian when I knew her. All I had was "churchianity," which never saved anyone.)

I even pray for the salvation of Osamu Bin Laden, particularly since I understand why he hates the American government so much

– for ignoring the plight of the Palestinians, who were cheated out of their land. (After all, he said it was the Mid-East policy of America that caused him to become a terrorist.) Wouldn't it be wonderful if he were to come to the Lord Jesus and be totally changed by Him? He would be the most effective ex-Muslim evangelist on the planet, I think. And many would follow him to the Lord Jesus Christ.

Farewell, dear Reader. If you have stuck with me through all of this, I believe you have "hearing ears." Since I am 73 and had a slight stroke last year, I expect to be going Home to Heaven, soon. But I hope to see you, there. My husband and I shared our 51st anniversary, recently.

My prayer is that there will be one glorious reunion in heaven one day – and we shall meet you there!

Notes

Chapter One:

1. Alfred Lilienthal, *The Zionist Connection.* New York: Dodd, Mead, & Company, 1978, p.561.
2. Paul Findley, *They Dare to Speak Out.* Lawrence Hill Books, 814 N. Franklin St., Chicago, IL, 60610, p. 165.
3. Op. Cit., p. 166.
4. Op. Cit., p. 167.
5. Ibid.
6. Ibid.
7. Op. Cit., p. 168.
8. Lilienthal, Op. Cit., p. 565.
9. Findley, Op. Cit., p. 167.
10. Lilienthal, Op. Cit., p. 567.
11. Op. Cit., p. 566.
12. Op. Cit., p. 570.
13. Op. Cit., p. 568-9.
14. Findley, Op. Cit., pp. 175-6.
15. Op. Cit., pp. 173-4.
16. Op. Cit., p. 171.
17. Op. Cit., p. 170.
18. Op. Cit., p. 177.
19. Op. Cit., p. 174.
20. Ibid.
21. New York: *The Universal Jewish Encyclopedia, Vol. 6, 1942, p. 233.*
22. Ibid.
23. Ibid.
24. Richard Walker, "Spies in Pentagon Ignored," *American Free Press,* 9/13/04, p. 1.
25. Lilienthal, Op. Cit., p. 575.
26. *USA Weekend,* "Who's News?" 8/20, 2004, p.2.

27. Pat Brooks, *Hear, O Israel.* 2 Chronicles 7:14, Box 1212, Fairview, NC 28732, pp 111-12.

Chapter Two:
1. Genesis 16:16.
2. Genesis 17:15-16.
3. Genesis 17:19.
4. Genesis 21:10.
5. Genesis 21: 12 & 13.
6. Genesis 21: 17-19.
7. Genesis 24:60.
8. Genesis 22:1-14.
9. John 1:29.
10. Isaiah 53:4-6.
11. Psalm 22: 14-18.
12. 2 Corinthhians 5:21.
13. John 3:16.
14. I John 5:1.

Chapter Three:
1. Genesis 49:10.
2. Genesis 25:25 & 26.
3. Genesis 25:31-34.
4. Genesis 27:12 & 13.
5. Genesis 30:1
6. Genesis 30:22-24.
7. Genesis 31:35.
8. Matthew 12:36.
9. Genesis 32:8.
10. Genesis 32:9-12.
11. Genesis 32: 22, 23.
12. Genesis 32: 24.
13. Genesis 32:28.
14. Genesis 49: 17.
15. Genesis 48:19.

16. Benjamin Freedman, *Facts Are Facts,* reprinted in *Hear, O Israel,*by Pat Brooks. New Puritan Library, Box 1212, Fairview, NC 28730, 1981, p. 58. Disappeared from our library in 2004!

Chapter Four:
1. I Kings 11:6.
2. I Kings 11:30-32.
3. I Kings 12: 11.
4. I Kings 12:15.
5. I Kings 12:24
6. Wm. H. Poole, *Anglo-Israel, or the Saxon Race.* Toronto: William Briggs, 1881, p. 340.
7. Arnold C. Brackman, *The Luck of Ninevah.* New York: McGraw-Hillok Company, 1978, p. 115.
8. B.B. Kirkbridge Bible Company, Inc., *Thompson Chain Reference Study Bible,* 10th printing, March 1977, Archeological Supplement, p.. 1721.
9. Poole, Op. Cit., p. 138.
10. Merrill F. Unger, *Unger's Bible Dictionary.* Chicago: Moody Press, 1957, p. 809.
11. Poole, Op. Cit., p. 132.
12. *Op. Cit.,* pp. 136-37.
13. *Ibid.*
14. Bukdahl, Jorgen, et al, *Scandinavia, Past & Present.* Ankrone, Denmark, 959, p. 45..
15. Poole, *Op. Cit.,* p. 113.
16. Hosea 1:6 & 7.
17. Unger, *Op. Cit,* p. 591.
18. Hosea 1:6 & 7.
19. Hosea l:9-11.
20. Hosea 12: 1.
21. Hosea 6:1-3.
22. 2 Peter 3:8.

Chapter Five:
1. Matthew 27:28
2. Claude G. Montefiore, quoted by Chief Rabbi Stephen S. Wise, in *Sermons & Addresses, Vol. II.* New York: Bloch Publishing Co, 1910, p.72.
3. Arsene Darmesteter, article on *The Talmud,* original published in French in Quarterly Review, translated by Henrietta Szold, 1897.
4. *Revelation 2:8-11*
5. *Revelation 3:7-12.*
6. *Ephesians 2:8 & 9*
7. "Kol Nidre," *The Jewish Encyclopedia, Vol. VII. NY & London: Funk & Wagnalls Co., 1904, p. 8*
8. *Deuteronomy 23:21.*
9. Pat Brooks, *Hear, O Israel.* Fairview, NC: New Puritan Library, 1981, reprint of *Facts are Facts (booklet Freedman, which has disappeared from our library).*

Chapter Six:
1. *A Call To War, by Pat Brooks. NPL, Box 1212,* Fairview, NC, 1985, pp. 21-25
2. Rev. 6:4
3. Heb. 12:16 & 17
4. Malachi 1: 1-4.
5. Romans 9:13.
6. "Edom," *Encyclopedia Judaica, Vol. 6.* Jerusalem: *EncyclopediaJudaica Company, 1971, p.378.*
7. "Edom, Idumea," *The Jewish Encyclopedia, Vol. V. NY &* London: Funk & Wagnalls Company, 1804, p.41.
8. "Edom (Idumea)", *The New Standard Jewish Encyclope*den City, NY: Doubleday & Co., 1977, p. 378.
9. Flavius Josephus, *The Antiquities of the Jews. Grand* Rapids, MI: Kregel *Publications, p. 279.*
10. Unpublished Ms. of Charles W. Ewing, from *Hear, O Israel,* by Pat Brooks. Fairview, NC: NPL, 1981, p. 153.

11. Psalm 11:3.
12. Geo. Washington, quoted by J.F. Schroeder, *Maxims of Washington.* NY: D.Appleton & Co., 1894, p.243.

Chapter Seven:
1. Pat Brooks, *A Call to War.* NPL, Box 1212, Fairview, NC 28730, 1985, p. 49.
2. Pat Brooks, *Return of the Puritans.* NPL, Box 1212, Fairview, NC 28730, 1983, p. 59.
3. Op. Cit., pp. 60-62.
4. Op. Cit., pp. 62-63.
5. Op. Cit., p. 68.
6. Ibid.
7. Op. Cit., p. 69.
8. Op. Cit., p. 70.
9. Numbers 30:2.
10. Hebrews 10:26.
11. Galatians 3:16
12. Galatians: 3: 28 & 29
13. Alfred M. Lilienthal, *The Zionist Connection.* NY: Dodd, Mead, & Co., 1978, p. 14.
14. Op. Cit, pp. 18 & 19
15. Op. Cit., p. 27.
16. Op. Cit., p. 33
17. Op. Cit., p. 34
18. Ibid.
19. Op. Cit., p. 35.
20. Ibid.
21. Op. Cit., p. 40.
22. Op. Cit., p. 483
23. Op. Cit., p. 484.
24. Matthew 7:21-23.
25. Martin Luther, *The Jews & Their lies,* Liberty Bell Publications, Reedy, WV, pp. 63 & 64.
26. Proverbs 29:25.
27. Lilienthal, Op. Cit., p.156.
28. "The Phony War on Terrorism," by Des Griffin, quoting *"Yol Yisrael,"* *mediabypass.com, 4/03, pp. 39&40.*
29. *American Free Press, 645 Pennsylvania Ave., S.E.,* Washington, DC 20001, *10/20/04 , p.2.*
30. Matthew 5:13.
31. Romans 3:23.
32. John 3:16.

Bibliography

1. Barton, David, *Original Intent.* Wall Builders, 426 Circle Drive, Aledo, TX 76008, 2000.
2. Findley Paul, *They Dare to Speak Out.* Lawerence Hill Books, an imprint of Chicago Review Press, Inc. 814 No. Franklin St., Chicago, IL 60610, 1989.
3. Graham, Dr. O.J., *The Six-Pointed Star.* The Free Press 777, Box 452, Don Mills, Ont. M3C 2T2, Canada, 2000.
4. Griffin, Des, *Descent into Slavery?* Emissary Publications, 9205 Clackamas Rd., Clackmas, OR 97015, 1996.
5. Koestler, Arthur, *The Thirteenth Tribe.* New York: Random House, 1976.
6. Lilienthal, Alfred M., *The Zionist Connection.* New York: Dodd, Mead, & Co., 1978.
7. Lloyd, James, *The Lion, the Bear, & The Leopard.* Christian Media Network, P.O. Box 448, Jacksonville, OR 97530.
8. Poch, Ron, *I WANT To Be Left Behind.* Liberty Press, Box 339, Adrian, MI 49221, 2002.
9. Reed, Douglas, *The Controversy of Zion.* Dolphin Press, Ltd., Box 3145, Durban, Natal, S.A., 1978.
10. Rittenhouse, Stan, *For Fear of the Jews.* The Exhorters, Box 492, Vienna, VA 22180, 1982.
11. Weiland, Ted, *God's Covenant People,* Mission to Israel, Box 248, Scottsbluff, NE 699363,1994.
12. Poole, William H., *Anglo-Israel, or the Saxon Race.*

Toronto: William Briggs, 1881. This book is out of print, and has been for decades. However, the research & Biblical insights it contains must be preserved. We urge readers who agree to contact individuals or foundations who may wish to put it back into print, and pray with us that it shall be available soon. Right now, it is available only on inter-library loan. There are only 40 copies left in America.

Being a brief consideration
of the distinctions between
the great Biblical principles
on which the
American constitutional republic
was founded
and the malignant doctrines
of "democracy"
into which this nation has fallen.

(Reprinted by permission of the Plymouth Rock Foundation, P.O. Box 425, Marlborough, NH 03455.)

REPUBLIC

GOVERNMENT BASED ON GOD'S LAW

Bible is textbook of govt. Law based on God's law. Constitution guarantees individual freedom, defines proper functions of govt. Minority rights upheld (Ex 20:1-17, 24:3; Dt 4:1-9, 17:18-19; Isa 33:22; Gal 5:1.)

REPRESENTATIVE GOVERNMENT

Power flows from God to citizen to representatives. People elect legislators, executives, judges. Officials accountable to electorate. Rights & due process upheld. (Ex 18:19-25, 19:5-8; Lev 19:15; Dt 1:13-18, 16:18-20; Rom 13:1-4; Tim 3:1-13.)

LIMITED GOVERNMENT

God is Sovereign; govt. His minister of justice. Citizens restrict govt. power, divide it between fed, state & local levels, erect checks & balances. (Num 16:1-3; Dt 10:12-14, 11:1; Josh 22:14; Ps 22:28; Acts 5:29, 17:7; Rom 13:3-4; 1 Tim 6:15.)

DEMOCRACY

MAN'S GOVERNMENT (Humanism)

State is "god," "vox populi" is sovereign. Majority rule, minority rights suppressed. God's law denied, humanism is state "religion." (1 Sam 8:7; 2 Chron 7:19-22; Isa 1:21-26; Mk 7:20-23; Rom 1: 21-25, 8:7.)

DIRECT GOVERNMENT (Mobocracy)

The people rule by emotion, legislate on impulse, judge by vote. No absolutes. Reason replace righteousness, majority decrees "justice." (Gen 11:1-9; Ex 23:1-2; Judges 21:25; Isa 59:1-15.)

CENTRALIZED GOVERNMENT (Tyranny)

Federal govt. unrestrained, local govts. mere appendages. Controls and bureaucracies sap nation's resources. Caesar is arbiter of morals, "truth" is what serves State (1 Sam 8:14-18; Isa 3:1-15; John 19:15.)

88

REPUBLIC

PROPERTY RIGHTS SECURE

All property is God's, entrusted to individuals as His vice regents. Man has property in self, in rights & estate. Govt's function is to protect person and property (Ex 20:15-17, 22:3, 30:15; Lev 27:30-33; Num 5:6-8; Ps 24:1; 1 Cor 10:26.)

INDIVIDUAL LIBERTY (Freedom)

Liberty is gift from God to be exercised within His laws. Basic law of liberty is Ten Commandments. Mt 22 37-40, and to be conscientious toward God (Ex 20:2; John 8:36; Acts 24:16; Gal 5:13; 1 Pet 2:16.)

STEWARDSHIP (Free Enterprise)

God created man to glorify Him & to tend His earth. Man is God's steward, to be fruitful, to fulfill God's dominion charter and to obey His work rules (Gen 1:18; 3; Lev 27:30-33; Dt 25.4; Mt 6:21,33; 25:14-20; Eph 6:5-8.)

DEMOCRACY

TAXATION (Confiscation)

Taxation an instrument of social control, citizens made servants of State. Personal property progressively taxed to support Caesar's excesses. (Lev 19:13; 1 Sam 8:11-18; 1 Kings 21:1-19.)

LICENSE

Liberty licensed by majority; minority must conform. "Broad public policy" is "god," constitutional guarantees give way to concensus and "divine right" of public officials. (2 Pet 2:17-19; Jude 4,5; Rev 17&18).

COLLECTIVISM (Socialism)

Materialism is worshipped. Govt controls production & distribution. Man must serve State, not God. Property a privilege conferred or cancelled by State (Lk 12:13-21; Rev 13:16-17.)

The Fall and Rising Again of Israel

"And Simeon blessed them, and said unto Mary his mother, 'Behold, this child is set for the fall and rising again of many in Israel, and for a sign which shall be spoken against.'" (Luke 2:34)

The Fall		The Rising Again	
Isaiah	3:24, 25	Isaiah	44:26
	8:13, 14		49:5-10
	28:13		52:1-7
Jeremiah	6:21		58-4-12
	8:12		60:1-5
Ezekiel	6:1-7		61:4-9
	6:11, 12	Ezekiel	34:28-31
	11:8-12	Hosea	3:5
Hosea	4:5		6:1, 2
	5:5	Joel	2:18-27
	13:16	Amos	9:11
	14:1	Micah	4:11-13
Amos	7:17	Romans	11:11, 15
Micah	7:7-9		11:22-27
		I Peter	2:6-10

— *Compiled by W. Roger Rusk, late Professor of Physics, University of Tennesse.*

APPENDIX C

The Divided Kingdom

	Northern	Southern
1. Common Name	Israel	Judah
2. Corporate Name	House of Israel	House of Judah
3. Covenant Name	House of Joseph	House of David
4. Poetic Name	Ephraim	Zion
5. Number of Tribes	Ten	Two + Levites
6. Capital City	Samaria	Jerusalem
7. Dynasties	Nine	One (David)
8. Duration	250 Years	390 Years
9. First King	Jeroboam	Rehoboam
10. Last King	Hoshea	Zedekiah
11. Primary Worship	Calves, Baal	Jehovah, Baal
12. Place of Worship	Dan and Bethel	Jerusalem
13. Captivity	Assyria, 722 BC	Babylon, 586 BC
14. Prophet of Judgment	Hosea, Amos	Jeremiah
15. Prophet of Hope	Isaiah	Isaiah
16. Raw Material	Potter's Clay	Broken Bottle
17. Metaphor	Vine	Figs
18. Final OT State	Divorced	Unfaithful
19. History	II Kings 17	II Chronicles 36
20. Promise	Many Seed	One Seed
21. Inheritance	Birthright	Sceptre
22. Appointment	Kingdom	Throne
23. Function	Dominion	Sanctuary
24. World Identity	Gentiles	Jews
25. Destiny	My People	My Praise

— Compiled by W. Roger Rusk

Table Of Indo-European Languages

TABLE OF INDO-EUROPEAN LANGUAGES

Division	Subfamily	Branch	Group	Languages and Dialects *	Chief Locality †
EASTERN OR SATEM	INDO-IRANIAN or ARYAN	Indic	Sanskritic	*Sanskrit (Vedic, Classical); Pali; Prakrit;* including *Avanti, Maharashtri, Magadhi (Ardhamagadhi), Sauraseni;;* Kashmiri, ‡Kohistani, ‡Lahnda (Jatki, Multani), Sindhi; Marathi (Konkani); Oriya, Bihari (Bhojpuri, Magahi, Maithili); Bengali, Assamese;; Eastern Hindi (Awadhi, Baheli);; Western Hindi (Hindustani, incl. Urdu, Dakhini, Braj Bhasha, Bundeli, Kanauji), Rajasthani (Marwari, Jaipuri), Gujarati (Bhili), Panjabi; Pahari (Khas, Garhwali); Singhalese, Romany or Gypsy	India
			Dard or Pisaca	Shina, Khowar, Kafiri	Chitral, Kafiristan, etc.
		Iranian	East	Afghan or Pashto; Baluchi; Galcha	Afghanistan, Baluchistan, etc.
			West	*Avestan, Old Persian, Middle Persian (Pahlavi, Pazend, Parsi, Huzvaresh),* Modern Persian: Kurdish; *Scythian,* Ossetic	Persia, Kurdistan, Caucasia
	THRACO-PHRYGIAN or ANATOLIC	Phrygian		*Phrygian*	Ancient Phrygia
		Armenian		Armenian *(Old* or *Classical,* Modern)	Armenia
	THRACO-ILLYRIAN			*Thracian, Illyrian,* Albanian (Gheg, Tosk)	Balkan Peninsula
	BALTO-SLAVIC	Slavic or Slavonic	South	*Church Slavic* or *Old Bulgarian;* Bulgarian, Serbo-Croatian (Serbian, Croatian), Slovenian	Bulgaria, Yugoslavia
			East or Russian	Great Russian or Russian, White Russian, Little Russian or Ukrainian	Russia
			West	Czechoslovak (Czech, Moravian, Slovak); Sorbian or Wendish; Polish, Kasubian, *Polabian*	Czechoslovakia, Poland, Germany
		Baltic or Lettic		*Old Prussian,* Lithuanian, Lettish	East Prussia, Lithuania, Latvia
WESTERN OR CENTUM	HELLENIC	Greek		*(Old Ionic* or *Epic, New Ionic, Attic; Doric; Aeolic,* including *Boeotian, Lesbian, Thessalian; Arcadian, Elean, Cyprian),* Modern Greek (Romaic; Neo-Hellenic)	Greece and Asia Minor
	ITALIC	Osco-Umbrian		*Oscan; Umbrian*	Italy
		Sabellian		*(Aequian, Marrucinian, Marsian, Paelignian, Sabine, Vestinian, Volscian)*	
		Latinian	Latin and Romance	*(Faliscan, Lanuvian, Praenestinian)* *Latin; langue d'oïl, langue d'oc,* French, Provençal, Franco-Provençal, Catalan; Spanish (Andalusian, Aragonese, Asturian, Castilian, Leonese), Portuguese (Galician); Italian (Tuscan or standard Italian); Rhaeto-Romanic (Romansh, Ladin, Friulian); Rumanian	Italy, France, Spain, Portugal, Switzerland, Rumania
	CELTIC	Continental		*Gaulish*	Ancient Gaul
		Insular	Cymric or Brythonic	*Cornish,* Welsh, Breton	Cornwall, Wales, Brittany
			Goidelic	Irish, Gaelic, Manx	Ireland, Scotland, Isle of Man
	TEUTONIC or GERMANIC	East		*Gothic*	Ancient Germany, etc.
		North or Scandinavian		*Old Norse,* Icelandic, Swedish, Danish, Norwegian	Scandinavia
		West	High	*Old High German (Frankish* in part, *Alamannic, Bavarian), Middle High German,* German	Germany, Austria
			Low	*Old Saxon, Old Low Frankish,* Low German or Plattdeutsch, Dutch, Flemish, Frisian *Anglo-Saxon, Middle English,* English (Scottish)	Germany, Holland, Belgium, England, etc.

* Semicolons [;] divide subgroups; double semicolons [;;], major subgroups; parentheses [( )] indicate dialects. Italics show dead languages.
† Localities where Indo-European languages have been carried in recent times by immigration, as North America for English, Spanish America for Spanish, are not here indicated. ‡ With a Dardic basis.